what is
philosophy?

what is
philosophy?

a guide to the world of thought and logic

gary hayden

METRO BOOKS
New York

METRO BOOKS
New York

An Imprint of Sterling Publishing Co., Inc.
1166 Avenue of the Americas
New York, NY 10036

ISBN 978-1-4351-5973-0

For information about custom editions, special sales, and
premium and corporate purchases, please contact
Sterling Special Sales at 800-805-5489
or specialsales@sterlingpublishing.com.

Manufactured in China

2 4 6 8 10 9 7 5 3 1

www.sterlingpublishing.com

Design and illustration by Simon Daley

Conceived, designed, and produced by
Quid Publishing
Part of The Quarto Group
Level 4 Sheridan House
114 Western Road
Hove BN3 1DD
England

www.quidpublishing.com

contents

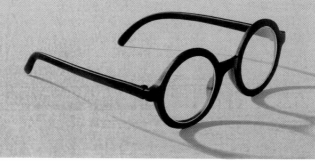

introduction

In our more reflective moments, we may find ourselves pondering life's big questions. Take any of the following, for instance:

Why are we here?
Why does the universe exist?
How ought we to live?
Is there a God?
How dependable are our beliefs?
Is the world purely physical—or is there a nonphysical aspect to it too?

Questions like these are the subject-matter of philosophy. Plato, history's most famous philosopher, said that philosophy begins in wonder.

Looking at the kinds of questions that philosophy investigates, you can see why. They're the kinds of questions you could spend your whole life contemplating, and still feel unsure about the answers.

In fact, they're the kinds of questions to which definitive answers may never be found. But in philosophy the questions are just as important as the answers.

In the words of the twentieth-century English philosopher, Bertrand Russell (1872–1970): "These questions enlarge our conception of what is possible, enrich our intellectual imagination, and diminish the dogmatic assurance which closes the mind against speculation."

However, it's important to note that philosophy only begins in wonder. After that, there's thinking to be done. A lot of thinking.

If you were to sit beneath the stars on a wonderful summer evening, sipping on a glass of wine and idly pondering the mysteries of existence, you would be doing something pleasant and worthwhile. But you wouldn't really be doing philosophy. This is because philosophy is not characterized by its subject-matter alone, but also by its method. And its method is logical, analytical, critical, reflective, painstaking, imaginative and open-minded.

Philosophers don't take intellectual short-cuts. They never assume that a point of view is right merely because it seems plausible. And they never assume that a point of view is wrong merely because it seems implausible. Instead they explore topics from every conceivable angle, considering all of the relevant arguments, and following wherever those arguments lead. This means that philosophy is excellent mental training.

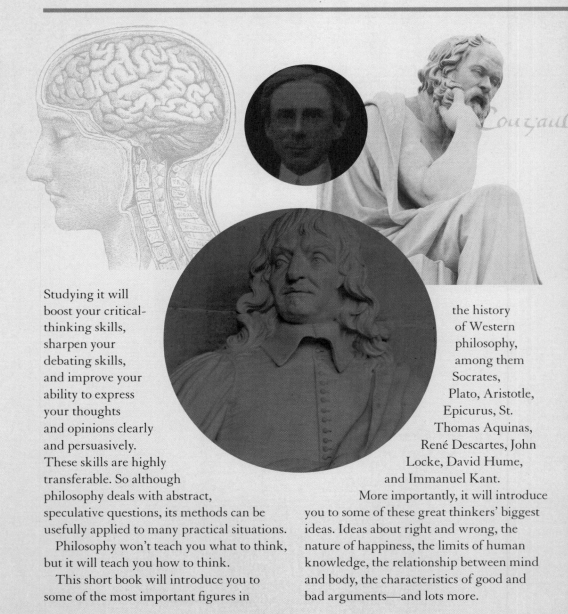

Studying it will boost your critical-thinking skills, sharpen your debating skills, and improve your ability to express your thoughts and opinions clearly and persuasively. These skills are highly transferable. So although philosophy deals with abstract, speculative questions, its methods can be usefully applied to many practical situations.

Philosophy won't teach you what to think, but it will teach you how to think.

This short book will introduce you to some of the most important figures in the history of Western philosophy, among them Socrates, Plato, Aristotle, Epicurus, St. Thomas Aquinas, René Descartes, John Locke, David Hume, and Immanuel Kant.

More importantly, it will introduce you to some of these great thinkers' biggest ideas. Ideas about right and wrong, the nature of happiness, the limits of human knowledge, the relationship between mind and body, the characteristics of good and bad arguments—and lots more.

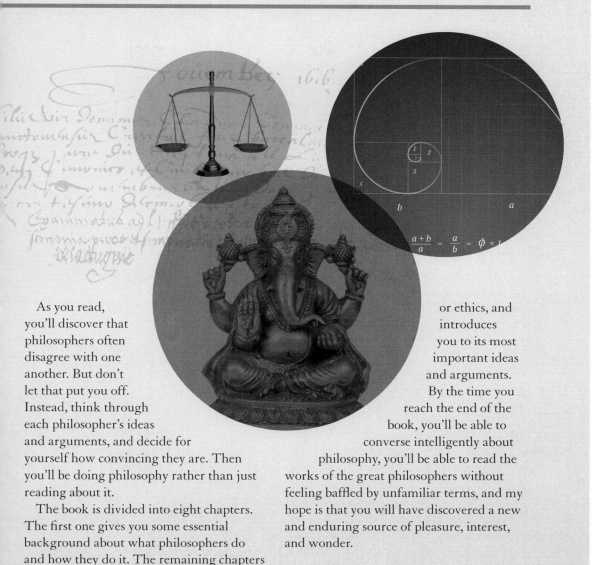

$$\frac{a+b}{a} = \frac{a}{b} = \phi \approx 1$$

As you read, you'll discover that philosophers often disagree with one another. But don't let that put you off. Instead, think through each philosopher's ideas and arguments, and decide for yourself how convincing they are. Then you'll be doing philosophy rather than just reading about it.

The book is divided into eight chapters. The first one gives you some essential background about what philosophers do and how they do it. The remaining chapters are organized thematically. Each one takes a philosophical topic, for example logic or ethics, and introduces you to its most important ideas and arguments.

By the time you reach the end of the book, you'll be able to converse intelligently about philosophy, you'll be able to read the works of the great philosophers without feeling baffled by unfamiliar terms, and my hope is that you will have discovered a new and enduring source of pleasure, interest, and wonder.

—Gary Hayden

what is philosophy?

deep
questions

What is philosophy? This is a notoriously difficult question. If you asked it of 20 different philosophers you would probably get 20 different answers—and all of them correct! Asking "What is philosophy?" is a bit like asking "What is love?" Love is a messy, multifaceted thing. It can't be summed up in a neat definition. The only way to understand it is to encounter it in all of its different forms and guises.

Philosophy, too, is a messy, multifaceted thing that resists simple definitions and needs to be experienced to be understood. This means that you won't really begin to understand what philosophy is all about until you get to the end of this book. But we can take a first small step by looking at a dictionary definition.

philosophy defined

The *Oxford Dictionary* defines philosophy as "the study of the fundamental nature of knowledge, reality, and existence, especially when considered as an academic discipline." Like many definitions of philosophy, this one is perfectly correct, as far as it goes. But anyone unacquainted with the subject may struggle to make sense of "the fundamental nature of knowledge, reality, and existence."

What does it mean? Well, it means that philosophy is concerned with the deepest, most fundamental questions that can be asked about the world, about the nature of things, and about our knowledge of those things. Philosophers wrestle with big questions—ones that get to the very heart of things—such as "Why does the universe exist?", "Is there a God?", and "Can we know anything with absolute certainty?"

Questions like these are baffling. They can make your brain hurt. It can be difficult even to know how to make a start on them. You won't find the answers to such questions by looking through a microscope, or by doing an experiment, or by conducting a survey. All you can do is reflect upon them, think hard about them, and bring all of your powers of reason to bear upon them. Even then, you're unlikely to come up with definitive answers.

Whatever conclusions you reach, you'll find, as you discover more about philosophy, that some of history's most profound thinkers had very good reasons for reaching entirely opposite conclusions.

a sense of wonder

Philosophy is unlike most academic subjects in that it doesn't have many right answers, as such. In philosophy, there are opinions supported by arguments, and there are other, sometimes contradictory, opinions supported by other arguments. So, given that there are few right answers in philosophy, why study it?

One reason is that philosophical questions, however baffling and frustrating, are so damned fascinating. Those of us who are philosophically inclined just can't help pondering the deepest questions about life, the universe, and everything.

In the following passage, taken from his dialogue, *Theaetetus*, the Greek philosopher Plato (427–347 BCE) makes this point very eloquently:

THEAETETUS: *Yes, Socrates, I stand in amazement when I reflect on the questions that men ask. By the gods, I do! I want to know more and more about such questions, and there are times when I almost become dizzy just thinking about them.*

SOCRATES: *Ah, yes, my dear Theaetetus, when Theodorus called you a philosopher he described you well. That feeling of wonder is the touchstone of the philosopher, and all philosophy has its origins in wonder.*

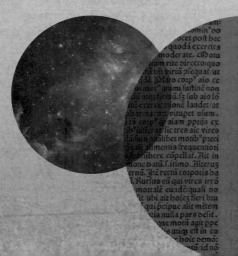

clear thinking

Although there aren't many right answers in philosophy, and although philosophers often disagree with one another, that doesn't mean that philosophy is a mere free-for-all of ideas. In fact, one of the most distinctive features of philosophy is its commitment to intellectual justification—to clear, logical thinking.

When presenting an idea or a solution to a philosophical problem, philosophers must offer supporting arguments. Note that argument here doesn't mean quarrel. It means a series of statements offering reasons for accepting a particular conclusion.

Philosophers spend a lot of time building, examining, criticizing, and demolishing arguments. So, far from being a free-for-all of ideas, philosophy is a discipline where everything has to be justified in a reasoned and logical manner.

However, it's important to note that logic isn't the be-all and end-all of philosophy.

Arguments containing logical slips or those built upon fuzzy thinking generally get dismissed quickly—but that isn't to say that arguments built upon impeccable logic will necessarily be successful.

Impeccable logic isn't always—indeed, often isn't—a guarantee of truth, as the following example shows:

All dogs are boys, and all cats are girls.
Tiddles is a cat.
Therefore Tiddles is a girl.

The logical progression of this argument is faultless. But it's built upon a false premise—in reality, not all dogs are boys nor all cats girls—and therefore the conclusion may not be true. Despite being a cat, Tiddles might not be a girl.

That was a trite example. Here is a more philosophical one, taken from the pen of the great Scottish philosopher David Hume (1711–76): "[God's] power we allow infinite: whatever he wills is executed: but neither man nor any other animal is happy: therefore he does not will their happiness."

Hume is arguing against the notion of an all-powerful god who wishes happiness for his creatures. His reasoning is excellent:

God is said to have infinite power.
If that's the case, then whatever he wants to happen will happen.
But many of God's creatures are unhappy.
Therefore God must not want them to be happy.

Despite Hume's impeccable logic, it's possible to reject his argument. One way of doing this would be to deny the premise that God's infinite power necessarily means that everything he wants to happen will happen. He might, for example, have granted his creatures free will—including the ability to act contrary to his own wishes.

In this case, it's not the logic of Hume's argument that comes under fire, as such, rather one of the assumptions upon which his argument is built.

The upshot of this is that when you read what a philosopher has to say on a given subject, you shouldn't necessarily interpret him as saying, "Here's some air-tight logic that proves my point beyond all doubt." Instead, you might think of his approach as, "I've given this matter a great deal of thought, and I've come to certain conclusions. And if you follow my train of thought and give the matter some serious consideration yourself, I think you'll come to agree with me."

philosophy's distinctive methods

In the following quote, taken from his book *The Problem of Knowledge*, the English philosopher A. J. Ayer (1910–89) describes philosophy's methods. He makes three key points, which will, by now, be familiar to you: 1) philosophers rely heavily on reasoned argument; 2) philosophical theories can't be tested by observation; and 3) philosophical proofs seldom have the kind of logical certainty that mathematical proofs have.

It is by its methods rather than its subject matter that philosophy is to be distinguished from other arts and sciences. Philosophers make statements which are intended to be true, and they commonly rely on argument both to support their own theories and to refute the theories of others; but the arguments which they use are of a very peculiar character. The proof of a philosophical statement is not, or is only seldom, like the proof of a mathematical statement; it does not normally consist in formal demonstration. Neither is it like the proof of a statement in any of the descriptive sciences. Philosophical theories are not tested by observation.

appearance & reality

So far, we have learned that philosophy is about applying clear logical thinking to deep and difficult questions. One such philosophical question is "What's the relationship between appearance and reality?" Or, putting it slightly differently, "Is the way things *appear to be* how they *really are*?"

To illustrate some clear thinking upon this question, I will follow a line of thought developed in the opening chapter of *The Problems of Philosophy*, a classic introductory text written by the British philosopher Bertrand Russell (1872–1970).

Russell begins by asking: "Is there any knowledge in the world, which is so certain that no reasonable man could doubt it?"

Our first response to this question might be to say that we can't reasonably doubt the evidence of our own present sensory experience. I might claim, for example, that I can be certain that I'm currently sitting at a table, in a coffee shop, typing these words onto my laptop. The table is in front of me. It's dark brown in color, rectangular in shape, and smooth and solid to the touch. None of this can reasonably be doubted, as the evidence is right there before me.

A little thought, however, reveals that things are not as simple as they appear. Take color, for example. At first sight, the table seems to be a uniform shade of brown. But careful observation reveals that different parts appear to be very different colors according to how the light reflects from them. And the various patches of color seem to move around as I shift my viewpoint.

Furthermore, I know that if I were to look at the table in dim light, or under colored lights, or while wearing sunglasses, it would appear to be a very different hue than it is now. Clearly then, the color of the table depends not only upon the table itself but also on the way the light affects its surface and upon the spectator.

Next, consider texture. As I look at it now, the surface of the table appears smooth. But, if I were to examine it with a magnifying glass, I would see that its surface is actually somewhat bumpy. And if I used a microscope it would be revealed as a mass of hills, valleys, and jagged edges.

So what's the table *really* like? Is it rough or smooth? I'm tempted to say that what I see in the microscope corresponds more closely to what the table is really like than what I see with the naked eye. But, as Russell points out, if we can't trust what we see with the naked eye, why should we trust what we see through a microscope?

When it comes to shape, I seem to be on firmer ground. After all, the table top is clearly rectangular. And surely that's *always* the case. But, when I consider the matter further, I realize that from most viewpoints the table top doesn't actually *look* rectangular. Viewed from directly overhead or directly underneath it appears rectangular enough, but from any other point of view, perspectival effects come into play.

For example, from my current viewpoint, the furthest edge of the table appears shorter than the nearest edge, and the sides seem to slope inward the further back they go. So the "real" shape of the table isn't what I see. The "real" shape is something I *infer* from what I see. Once again, appearance is not the same as reality.

reality

As a result of such musings, Russell concludes: "It becomes evident that the real table, if there is one, is not the same as what we immediately experienced by sight or touch or hearing. The real table, if there is one, is not immediately known to us at all, but must be an inference from what is immediately known."

Notice that Russell twice uses the phrase "if there is one." This element of doubt regarding the existence of the real table may seem a bit far-fetched at this stage. But, as we will see in chapter 3, a little further thought about the table, and about the way we perceive it, justifies this note of philosophical caution.

For now, we can simply note that what seemed like a simple question has opened up a whole can of worms. Careful thought has revealed that the relationship between appearance and reality is far more complex than we originally took it to be.

dialogue

Philosophers can't just pluck ideas from the air and expect others to take them seriously. They must provide supporting arguments. They have to give reasons.

When offering a solution to a problem, philosophers invite criticism from their peers. They explain the problem they have tried to solve, offer their solution, and give a clear statement of their supporting arguments. This allows their peers to probe their understanding of the problem, test the logic and persuasiveness of their arguments, and assess the quality of their solution.

Philosophy, then, is a social endeavor. The stereotypical image of the philosopher alone, lost in thought, oblivious to the world, is misleading. Solitary musings can only take the philosopher so far. Sooner or later, their ideas and the reasoning behind them must be thrown open to debate.

For example, although the great French philosopher René Descartes (1596–1650) may have composed his 17th-century masterwork, *Meditations on First Philosophy*, in splendid isolation, he waited for feedback from other leading thinkers before publishing it. In fact, he included their most trenchant objections, together with his own replies, in the first published version.

Philosophers—even the greatest of them—need feedback. To quote the contemporary British philosopher and writer, Nigel Warburton: "Philosophy is an inherently social activity that thrives on the collision of viewpoints and rarely emerges from unchallenged interior monologue."

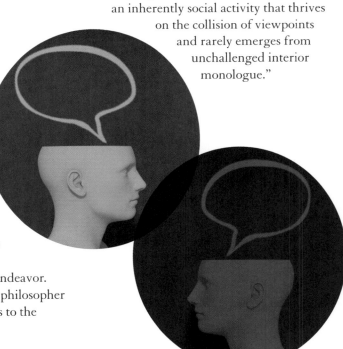

dialogue

And it's not just finished theories that get debated in philosophy. Most philosophical theories emerge and develop through dialogue. In fact, dialogue has been an integral part of the philosophical process ever since Western philosophy began, more than 2,000 years ago.

The Greek philosopher Socrates (ca. 470–399 BCE), who is often referred to as "the father of Western philosophy," was a passionate advocate of philosophy-through-dialogue. Occasionally he could be seen lost in solitary thought on the streets of Athens, but he was more commonly to be found debating philosophical questions with anyone who would listen.

Socrates believed that engaging in dialogue was the best way to challenge prejudices, stimulate new ideas, and develop thought. His strategy was to use skillful questioning to help his interlocutors identify the flaws in their existing concepts and to help them come up with better ones.

Socrates liked to think of himself as a midwife to other peoples' ideas, as Plato describes in his dialogue *Theaetetus*:

And the highest point of my art is the power to prove by every test whether the offspring of a young man's thought is a false phantom or instinct with life and truth… Those who frequent my company at first appear, some of them, quite unintelligent, but, as we go further with our discussions, all who are favored by heaven make progress at a rate that seems surprising to others as well as to themselves, although it is clear that they have never learned anything from me. The many admirable truths they bring to birth have been discovered by themselves from within. But the delivery is heaven's work and mine.

dialectic

Philosophers apply themselves to problems, and then offer solutions and supporting arguments. Other philosophers criticize those solutions and arguments and provide counterarguments and alternative solutions. This process is repeated over and over again in the hope that, over time, better and better solutions will emerge—or, failing that, that the nature of the problem will at least come to be better understood.

This exchange of arguments and ideas is known as "dialectic," a word that came to prominence in the works of Plato, who used it to label the method of discourse championed by Socrates in which people with different views try to establish the truth of a matter by means of reasoned argument. Over time, the word "dialectic" has acquired other connotations—in the philosophies of Immanuel Kant and Georg Wilhelm Friedrich Hegel, for example, and in the writings of Karl Marx and Friedrich Engels—but philosophers most often use the word in Plato's original sense.

branches of philosophy

Philosophy is traditionally divided into four main branches: logic, epistemology, metaphysics, and ethics.

This book will devote a lengthy chapter to each branch. For now, a brief overview will suffice.

logic

Logic is the study of right reasoning. It examines the structures and characteristics of good and bad arguments. If someone said, "Smoking can't be bad for you. My grandmother smoked 60 cigarettes a day and lived to be a hundred," they would show poor reasoning. Logic provides the tools to identify the weakness of such arguments, and far more complex and subtle ones.

Philosophers use the tools and methods of logic to test the ideas put forward in all of the other branches of philosophy.

epistemology

Epistemology is the branch of philosophy that deals with the nature and scope of human knowledge. It asks questions about what we can know and the methods by which we can come to know it.

When René Descartes shut himself up in an oven-heated room, determined to find out if there was any item of knowledge that was completely immune to doubt, he was engaging in an epistemological enquiry.

His famous insight that, doubt what he may, he couldn't possibly doubt his own existence—"I think, therefore I am"—has been hotly debated by philosophers ever since. Other epistemological questions include:

- **How is knowledge acquired?**
- **Are we born already knowing things, or are our minds a blank slate at birth?**
- **What's the difference between genuine knowledge and mere belief?**
- **By what methods do we acquire our beliefs? How reliable are those methods?**

metaphysics

Metaphysics is the study of existence and reality. It seeks to discover *what* there is and to understand the *nature* of what there is. For example, some philosophers (and many scientists) hold that everything that exists is, in some sense, material. In other words, that everything there is, including conscious experience, ultimately boils down to physics. Others argue that nonmaterial entities, such as God, the soul, numbers, the laws of physics, truth, and beauty also exist. Some deny the very existence of a material world, claiming that everything there is ultimately boils down to some aspect of mind or spirit.

Metaphysicians ponder such questions as:

- **Do we have free will, or is everything we do causally determined?**
- **What are numbers? Do they exist? If so, in what sense?**
- **What is a law of nature? How do we recognize one? Do they always apply?**
- **What is time? What is space?**
- **What is consciousness? What makes me, me—the same person I was yesterday?**

ethics

Ethics is concerned with values and with human action. It seeks the answers to questions relating to good and bad, right and wrong, and the purpose and meaning of life.

Socrates was intensely interested in ethical questions and claimed that every thinking person ought to be interested in them, too. He even went so far as to say that the unexamined life is not worth living.

Central questions in ethics include:

- **What makes some actions right and others wrong?**
- **Does life have meaning?**
- **What is happiness? How can it be achieved?**

Ethicists, or moral philosophers, also consider more specific questions, such as:

important subtopics

In addition to four lengthy chapters on logic, epistemology, metaphysics, and ethics, this book has some smaller chapters dealing with especially interesting and important subtopics of those disciplines.

philosophy of religion This is a branch of metaphysics that deals with questions regarding the nature and existence of God. It is also concerned with epistemological questions relating to religious experience and belief.

philosophy of mind This, too, is a branch of metaphysics. It probes the relationship between mind and body and seeks to understand the nature of consciousness and perception.

philosophy of science This is a branch of epistemology. It examines the characteristics, assumptions, methods, and implications of science.

- **Is capital punishment ever justified? If so, on what grounds?**
- **Is pornography wrong?**
- **Under what circumstances is civil disobedience justified?**
- **Under what circumstances is it morally permissible to abort a human fetus?**
- **Should we all be vegetarians?**

Socrates

Socrates is one of philosophy's most influential figures. To many people he represents the ideal of the philosopher, both intellectually and morally.

Although Socrates is called "the father of Western philosophy," he wasn't the first Western philosopher. Before him were the so-called pre-Socratics, such as Thales of Miletus, Pythagoras, Heraclitus, and Parmenides. These ground-breaking thinkers were not content with the mythological and supernatural explanations of existence that satisfied their contemporaries but trusted instead in reason and enquiry to unlock the world's secrets. They became known as philosophers from the Greek words *philo*, meaning love, and *sophia*, meaning wisdom.

The pre-Socratics were mostly interested in scientific problems such as "Where did everything come from?" and "What are the basic constituents of the world?"

enter Socrates

In the fifth century BCE, Socrates, a citizen of Athens, took philosophy in a new direction—he was more interested in people than physics. He applied the philosophers' method of critical enquiry to questions about men and women and their place in society, so laying the foundations of ethics.

Socrates was quite a character. He was, by all accounts, very unattractive: bulgy-eyed, bandy-legged, pot-bellied, and snub-nosed. And he adopted the peculiar practice of standing in the marketplace in Athens, engaging passers-by in debate. His favorite ploy was to ask an acknowledged expert for his opinion on some matter. Then, by skillful questioning, he would demonstrate that the "expert" knew very little. For example, he showed that an army general could give no satisfactory definition of courage and that a religious zealot could provide no coherent idea of holiness.

His intention was not to embarrass his opponents—although he frequently did— rather he was motivated by a desire for knowledge, and he believed that knowledge only emerges through a process of dialogue and systematic questioning.

the trial of Socrates

Socrates taught that right actions depend on right opinions and that each individual must take intellectual responsibility for forming those opinions. These notions proved unpopular with Athens's leaders, who preferred people to take their moral cues from the State. Socrates was put on trial, accused of introducing new gods and corrupting the youth of the city. He was found guilty and sentenced to death.

Refusing to plead for leniency, Socrates submitted to the death penalty by drinking hemlock. He died in an Athenian jail, surrounded by friends and admirers. The calm and dignified manner of his death is legendary and has inspired many works of art.

After Socrates's death, it was left to his star pupil, Plato, to carry the philosophical torch.

Plato's dialogues

Socrates never wrote anything down, so most of what we know about him comes to us through the writings of Plato. These are in the form of dialogues in which various characters explore philosophical topics by asking and answering questions of one another.

Socrates usually takes center stage in Plato's dialogues and invariably gets to display his razor-sharp debating skills, philosophical acumen, and moral integrity. Just how closely Plato's Socrates resembles the historical Socrates, both in terms of his character and his philosophical ideas, is not known, but no one doubts the historical Socrates's single-minded pursuit of wisdom, his commitment to clear thinking, or his zest for philosophical debate. He was, unquestionably, a philosopher *par excellence*.

Socrates in action

The best way to appreciate Socrates's approach to philosophy is to see him in action in one of Plato's dialogues.

In the following dialogue, which is known as the *Euthyphro*, Socrates is at court waiting to hear about some charges of "unholiness" that have brought against him by a young zealot named Meletus. While waiting, he gets into a discussion on the subject of holiness with an old friend of his, a priest named Euthyphro, who is at court to prosecute his own father on a charge of killing a slave.

What follows is an edited and condensed version of the early stages of their conversation, with some commentary from me:

lovers of wisdom

The early philosophers really were "lovers of wisdom." They believed that by the exercise of careful, systematic thought they could gain a deep understanding of the world and our place in it, thus becoming wise.

Philosophers nowadays tend to have more modest aspirations. Few would claim that their philosophical studies make them "wise" in the conventional sense. But in a more restricted sense, philosophers today might still be described as "lovers of wisdom' in that they have a profound respect for, and a strong commitment to, the careful exercise of reason.

SOCRATES: **Then tell me, what do you say the holy is? And what is the unholy?**

Euthyphro has previously declared himself an expert on holiness. So Socrates, not unreasonably, asks him to begin by explaining what holiness is.

EUTHYPHRO: **Well, I say that holy is doing what I am doing now, prosecuting murder and temple theft and everything of the sort, whether father or mother or anyone else is guilty of it. And not prosecuting is unholy.**

SOCRATES: **Try to answer more clearly the question I just asked. For, my friend, you did not sufficiently teach me before, when I asked you what the holy is; you said that the thing you are doing now is holy, prosecuting your father for murder.**

EUTHYPHRO: **Yes, and I told the truth, Socrates.**

SOCRATES: **Perhaps. But, Euthyphro, are there not many other things you say are holy, too?**

EUTHYPHRO: **Of course there are.**

SOCRATES: **Do you recall that I did not ask you to teach me about some one or two of the many things which are holy but about that characteristic itself by which all holy things are holy?**

Socrates objects that Euthyphro has not answered his question. He was asked to give a definition of holiness not to offer a specific example. Socrates complains that this is unsatisfactory since it offers no means of judging whether other acts are holy or not.

Euthyphro sees the justice of this complaint and offers a proper definition.

EUTHYPHRO: **Then what is dear to the gods is holy, and what is not dear to them is unholy.**

Socrates congratulates Euthyphro on having now given him a proper answer. But he raises an objection to it. The gods, he says, don't always feel the same way about things. So what is dear to one of them may not be dear to another. For example, although Zeus may approve of Euthyphro prosecuting his own father and consider it a holy act, Uranus may disapprove of it and consider it an unholy act.

EUTHYPHRO: **But I would certainly say that the holy is what all the gods love, and that the opposite, what all the gods hate, is unholy.**

Euthyphro modifies his definition and says that those acts are holy of which *all the gods* approve. By this stage, Euthyphro is sounding less sure of himself. But Socrates allows this new definition to stand for the moment and takes a different tack.

SOCRATES: **Now consider: is the holy loved by the gods because it is holy? Or is it holy because it is loved by the gods?**
EUTHYPHRO: **I do not know what you mean Socrates.**

Socrates spends some time explaining his meaning. What he wants to know is whether the gods love and approve of certain things because those things are, in themselves, holy, or are certain things to be considered holy *because* the gods love them.

Euthyphro is forced to admit that it must be the former.

SOCRATES: **Then it is loved because it is holy, not holy because it is loved?**
EUTHYPHRO: **It seems so.**
SOCRATES: **Then what is dear to the gods is not the same as holy, Euthyphro, nor is holy the same as dear to the gods, as you claim: the two are different.**

Euthyphro's definition of holiness is now in tatters. If the gods love the holy *because* it is holy, then being loved by the gods cannot be what *makes* it holy. By skillful questioning Socrates has enabled Euthyphro to understand that his existing view is flawed and that he now needs to come up with a better, more robust account of holiness.

Socrates's question "Is the holy loved by the gods because it is holy? Or is it holy because it is loved by the gods?" is known as the *Euthyphro* dilemma. It is discussed further in chapter 5 (see page 114).

Descartes

Just as Socrates is widely regarded as the father of Western philosophy, the 17th-century thinker René Descartes is generally considered the father of modern philosophy. His work marked a strong break with that of previous thinkers, whose authority he refused to accept, and has exerted an enormous influence on much subsequent philosophy.

Descartes was one of the leading intellectuals of his day—a great philosopher, a brilliant mathematician, and an accomplished scientist. Like many educated Europeans of his time, Descartes had been schooled in the Scholastic tradition, one which placed great reliance upon the authority of texts such as the Bible and the works of Aristotle.

Subsequently he had been exposed to new ways of thinking—the modern scientific conception of knowledge, with its emphasis on free enquiry and first-hand research, was emerging. Many of the old "certainties"—that Earth is the center of the universe, for example—were being questioned.

Descartes was at the cutting edge of this scientific revolution. He realized that much of what he had been taught in school was at best doubtful and at worst plain wrong. This realization stimulated him to embark on his own bold and brilliant philosophical quest to set all subsequent knowledge upon firm grounds.

the method of doubt

Taking mathematics as his inspiration, Descartes's idea was to begin with a few basic principles which were known, with absolute certainty, to be true and then, by meticulous reasoning and leaving not the slightest room for error, to rebuild the edifice of human knowledge.

The first step in this process was to pare knowledge to its bones, to refuse to accept any item of so-called knowledge that was open to even the slightest suspicion of doubt. To do this, he employed what has become known as the method of doubt.

The search for anything completely immune from doubt was far from easy. But Descartes did find something eventually. He found that, try as he might, he couldn't doubt his own existence. The very act of thinking about, and even trying to doubt, his own existence confirmed that he did, in fact, exist. Hence his famous dictum: "I think, therefore I am."

misconceptions

There is a common misconception about philosophers. They are thought by many people to spend most of their time concocting clever-sounding phrases with which to dazzle their disciples and admirers. This view is perfectly illustrated by a comment a friend of mine once made upon hearing Descartes's statement, "I think, therefore I am." He said, "If Descartes hadn't been such a big-name philosopher, I don't suppose anyone would have given those words a second thought."

He seemed to imagine that Descartes had woken up one morning, announced, quite out of the blue, "I think, therefore I am," and thus secured his place in philosophy's hall of fame. But that's far from the truth. The genius of "I think, therefore I am" can only be appreciated in the context of Descartes's method of doubt. It is the critical link in a complex and ingenious chain of argument that marked a watershed in the history of thought. Divorced from that context, it is a mere catchphrase.

A related misconception about philosophy is that the great philosophers have admirers and disciples who hang on their every word and who take all of their pronouncements as gospel. Again, this could hardly be further from the truth. I don't suppose there is any other class of people (with the possible exception of high-ranking politicians) whose ideas and arguments are so often scrutinized, criticized, debated, mauled, mangled, and rejected.

In fact, the very first lesson that the philosophy student learns is that nothing that Socrates, Plato, Aristotle, Epicurus, Marcus Aurelius, St. Augustine, St. Thomas Aquinas, Descartes, Locke, Berkeley, Hume, Kant, Hegel, Russell, or Wittgenstein says is to be taken on trust.

cogito ergo sum

what is logic?

reasons, logic & arguments

In chapter 1, we learned that philosophy is about applying clear logical thought to deep and difficult questions. Questions such as, "Why does something rather than nothing exist?" or "Does life have meaning?" and "Is the world really as it appears to be?" You won't find answers to questions like these by performing experiments or conducting surveys. All you can do is think long and hard about them and try to reason your way to answers that seem satisfactory.

Consider the ethical question of what makes some actions good and others bad. This can't be answered by observation. The goodness or badness of actions can't be seen, heard, felt, tasted, or smelled. Our only resource, then, is to think carefully about the concepts of good and bad, about how those concepts might apply in the ethical sphere, and about the kinds of actions that people tend to label good or bad. Then we must try to come up with a coherent and convincing theory to account for it all.

Many philosophers have done precisely that. And, as is so often the case in philosophy, they have come up with a variety of answers. For example, some philosophers have argued that actions should be considered good or bad according to their consequences. So actions that bring more pleasure than pain into the world can be considered good, while those that bring more pain than pleasure into the world can be considered bad.

For others, it's not the consequences of actions that makes them good or bad, rather the principles guiding them. So actions that conform to moral rules such as do not lie and do not kill can unequivocally be considered good, even though occasionally they might have harmful consequences.

Philosophers in both camps have their reasons for thinking the way they do. The question is, whose reasons are best?

logic

This is where logic comes in. Logic is the branch of philosophy concerned with good reasoning and with understanding what makes good reasoning good. Studying logic makes us better able to evaluate the reasons offered in support of given viewpoints and thereby enables us to make better-informed choices between competing views.

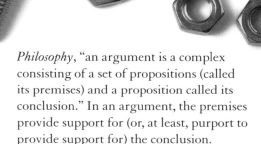

One way of putting it would be to say that logic is a tool—or a set of tools—to help us to assess the reasons for believing one thing rather than another. This is of fundamental importance in philosophy; it is also a highly transferable skill.

In our everyday lives we are bombarded every waking hour with reasons: reasons for voting a certain way, for subscribing to certain beliefs, for behaving in certain ways, for approving or disapproving of certain courses of action, for holding certain ideals, and so on. The methods and tools of logic make us better able to gauge the quality of those reasons.

So logic is useful to us not only when we study philosophy but whenever we read a newspaper, or listen to a politician's speech, or decide whether or not to support a cause—indeed, in any circumstance that calls for clear thinking.

arguments

In philosophy, the study of logic focuses very much on arguments. In fact, it's fair to say that arguments are the nuts and bolts of logic. They are to logic what numbers are to mathematics. But, whereas in everyday life the word "argument" is often used to mean quarrel or disagreement, in logic it is used very differently. In logic, an argument is a series of statements used to persuade someone of something or to present reasons for accepting a particular conclusion.

More formally, borrowing from the language of the *Oxford Companion to*

Philosophy, "an argument is a complex consisting of a set of propositions (called its premises) and a proposition called its conclusion." In an argument, the premises provide support for (or, at least, purport to provide support for) the conclusion.

Here's an example:

All Blue Party supporters are greedy and selfish.
Helen supports the Blue Party.
Therefore Helen is greedy and selfish.

The conclusion here is "Helen is greedy and selfish." The premises (reasons offered in support of this conclusion) are "All Blue Party supporters are greedy and selfish" and "Helen supports the Blue Party." Together, the premises and the conclusion constitute an argument.

Notice that the conclusion is preceded by the word "therefore." It is standard practice when setting out arguments in philosophy to mark the conclusion in this way, although "so" or "consequently" would do just as well.

When evaluating arguments, philosophers sometimes find it helpful to set them out in such a way that the arguments' premises and conclusions are clearly identified and labeled, as here:

PREMISE 1: **All Blue Party supporters are greedy and selfish.**
PREMISE 2: **Helen supports the Blue Party. Therefore**
CONCLUSION: **Helen is greedy and selfish.**

valid arguments

Every argument provides a statement of reasons in support of a conclusion. But those reasons may or may not be good reasons. There are bad as well as good arguments. The purpose of studying logic is to better enable us to distinguish between the two.

For example, this qualifies as an argument:

John goes to school on weekdays.
John is not a pupil.
Therefore John is a teacher.

But it clearly isn't a good one. It takes no account of the fact that John might be a janitor, administrator, or playground supervisor, etc.

The argument is constructed such that the premises don't lead logically to the conclusion. It's possible for the premises to be true at the same time that the conclusion is false. In philosophy, arguments of this nature are labeled invalid.

A valid argument, on the other hand, is one in which the premises *do* lead logically to the conclusion. It's impossible for the premises of a valid argument to be true but the conclusion false.

Here's an example of a valid argument:

All top-class soccer players are physically fit.
Britney Spears is a top-class soccer player.
Therefore Britney Spears is physically fit.

valid doesn't mean true

It may surprise some readers to learn that this argument *is* valid, since the second premise is clearly false. Britney Spears isn't a top-class soccer player. But—and this point is so important that it deserves to be written in bold type—**the validity of arguments has nothing whatsoever to do with whether they are true or not.**

An argument is valid if, and only if, it is constructed in such a way that the premises logically entail the conclusion. But that doesn't mean that either the premises or the conclusion must be true. It just means that they are related to one another in the right sort of way.

When assessing the validity of an argument, the key thing is to ask yourself, "If the premises *were* true, would the conclusion also have to be true?" If the answer is yes, then the argument is valid.

So, returning to the previous argument, we can see that if it *were* true that all top-class soccer players are physically fit, and if it *were* true that Britney Spears is a top-class soccer player, then logically it would follow that Britney Spears is physically fit. Therefore the argument is valid.

valid-looking invalid arguments

Invalid arguments can sometimes bear a close resemblance to valid ones. Consider, for example, the argument we saw earlier, which is perfectly valid:

All Blue Party supporters are greedy and selfish.
Helen supports the Blue Party.
Therefore Helen is greedy and selfish.

You might not think that it's a *good* argument, since you may take issue with the first premise. Nonetheless, the argument is valid since the premises, *if true*, guarantee the conclusion.

The following argument, however, is *invalid*:

All greedy and selfish people support
the Blue Party.
Helen supports the Blue Party.
Therefore Helen is greedy and selfish.

The small change in the wording of the first premise makes a world of difference to the quality of the argument. Stated this way, even if both premises of the argument were true, the conclusion might not be.

Even if it's true that all greedy and selfish people support the Blue Party, that doesn't necessarily mean that *only* greedy and selfish people support the Blue Party. Some nongreedy, nonselfish people may support them, too.

As my high-school math teacher used to say, "All cows are grass-eaters, but not all grass-eaters are cows."

an argument for everything

You can validly argue for *any* conclusion.

To prove it, let's take an outrageous statement, "Ringo was the most creative Beatle," and build a valid argument to support it.

Here goes:

The oldest member of the Beatles was also the most creative.
Ringo was the oldest Beatle.
Therefore Ringo was the most creative Beatle.

Here's another one:

Either Ringo Starr or George Harrison was the most creative Beatle.
George wasn't the most creative Beatle.
Therefore Ringo was the most creative Beatle.

One more, for good luck:

If Ringo Starr hadn't been the most creative member of the Beatles, he could never have written "Strawberry Fields Forever."
But Ringo did write "Strawberry Fields Forever."
Therefore Ringo was the most creative Beatle.

None of these is a sound argument. Each of them contains at least one untrue premise (for example, the one about Ringo writing "Strawberry Fields Forever"). Furthermore, the conclusion that all three arguments reach is clearly untrue.

But despite being riddled with untruths, all three arguments are valid. How so? Because *the validity of arguments has nothing whatsoever to do with whether they are true or not*.

All three arguments are constructed in such a way that *if* the premises were true then the conclusion would also, through logical necessity, be true. Therefore all three arguments, although unsound, are perfectly valid.

Validity has to do with the structure rather than the content of an argument. It's a matter of the premises and conclusion being related to one another in the right sort of way, logically speaking.

sound arguments

The fact that an argument is valid, then, is no guarantee that its conclusion is true. Validity guarantees only that *if* the premises are true *then* the conclusion must also be true. For an argument to be truly watertight it must not only be valid but also have true premises. Such arguments are labeled sound. The conclusion of a sound argument is always true.

Here's an example of a sound argument:

All bachelors are unmarried.
Paul is a bachelor.
Therefore Paul is unmarried.

And here's another one:

There's a dodo in the Oxford University Museum of Natural History.
There are no living dodos.
Therefore the Oxford dodo is not a living dodo.

In both cases, the premises are true; and in both the conclusion follows logically from the premises. So both arguments are sound.

It's worth noting, however, that there's an important difference between the two. In the first argument, the initial premise,

"All bachelors are unmarried," is absolutely, unequivocally, and indubitably true. All bachelors are, by definition, unmarried.

In the second argument, the second premise, "There are no living dodos," would be accepted as true for all everyday purposes. But it does suggest a very slight doubt. A really pernickety person might object that, for all we know, the dodo may not yet be extinct. There might be one or two of them still lurking around somewhere. This means that the creature I see before me might (no matter how unlikely) be a living dodo.

This slight but niggling doubt with the first premise means that, although the dodo argument almost certainly is sound, we can't be entirely sure that it is.

valid isn't enough

It's rarely enough for a philosopher—or for anyone else, for that matter—to demonstrate that his or her arguments are valid. It's possible to create any number of valid arguments for any conclusion, however absurd (see "an argument for everything" opposite).

Instead, a philosopher must try to show that his or her arguments are sound. That is, that they are properly reasoned arguments deriving from true premises.

For this reason, philosophers tend to spend as much time explaining and justifying the assumptions upon which their arguments are built as they do on the actual logic of those arguments.

deductive & inductive arguments

Arguments can be separated into two very distinct categories: deductive and inductive.

So far in this chapter, the arguments we've examined have all been what philosophers call deductive. Deductive arguments are those in which the premises logically entail the conclusion—or, at least, purport to do so.

As we have seen, some deductive arguments are valid, in which case the premises really *do* entail the conclusion, but others are invalid, in which case they don't.

A classic example of a valid deductive argument is:

All humans are mortal.
Socrates is human.
Therefore Socrates is mortal.

Anyone can see that if the premises are true (if all humans are indeed mortal and if Socrates is human) then it follows logically that the conclusion must be true, too.

A deductive argument is sound if, in addition to being valid, it has true premises. Sound arguments are the gold standard in deductive arguments, since their conclusions are guaranteed to be true.

inductive arguments

Not all arguments are deductive, though. Take this one, for instance:

No mayfly has ever been known to survive for two whole days.
Therefore none of the mayflies in the bell jar will survive for two whole days.

This is a very strong argument. If no mayfly has ever been known to survive for two whole days, it's highly unlikely that any fly in the bell jar will survive that long either. But there's no guarantee that one (or more) of them won't; the possibility is always there. Such arguments, in which true premises provide good reasons for accepting a conclusion but don't actually guarantee it, are known as inductive arguments.

from the particular to the general

Inductive reasoning usually moves from a limited number of specific observations to a general conclusion. For example, after observing the life cycle of thousands of mayflies, all of which died before they were two days old, we might reasonably conclude that mayflies never live for two whole days.

We can never be entirely sure that our general conclusion is true, but the more observations we make that confirm our theory the more confident we will become. It will only take one counterexample, however—a single observation of a 48-hour-old *Ephemeroptera*—to blow our theory apart.

induction in everyday life

We employ inductive reasoning all the time in our everyday lives. Indeed, we couldn't live without it. Every day, we make numerous assumptions that are necessary to our survival. We assume that water will quench our thirst, that food will nourish us, that sharp objects will harm us if we handle them carelessly, that collisions with cars and buses must be avoided, and so on.

In all of these cases we employ inductive reasoning. By way of example, we know that water has quenched our thirst many times in the past, and we induce (determine by induction) that it will continue to do so in future.

Inductive reasoning is also essential to science, as we shall discover in chapter 8.

the problem of induction

Inductive arguments, however strong, never logically entail their conclusions. So inductive reasoning can never lead to absolute certainty.

It doesn't matter how many observations we make, or how carefully we make them, or how consistently they yield the same result, there is always the logical possibility that the next observation may buck the trend.

This so-called "problem of induction" is a real bugbear for philosophers and will be discussed at length in chapter 8.

good and bad inductive arguments

The terms "valid" and "invalid" don't really apply to inductive arguments, since their premises never logically guarantee their conclusions. So, in that sense, all inductive arguments are invalid. But clearly some inductive arguments are better than others. Some give good grounds for accepting their conclusions. Others give poor grounds or no grounds at all. A good inductive argument is one in which the premises, if true, make it highly probable that the conclusion is also true.

argument forms

Logic is concerned with good reasoning, and with understanding what makes good reasoning good. More specifically, it is concerned with arguments and with understanding what makes arguments good or bad. We have already seen that one way in which arguments can be considered good is for them to be valid. That is, for their conclusions to follow logically from their premises.

In this section we examine some common forms of valid argument; in the following section we will examine some common forms of invalid argument. Familiarity with these will help you to recognize the validity of any given argument.

argument forms
Consider the following arguments:

If John has studied philosophy then he must have studied logic.

John *has* studied philosophy.
Therefore John must have studied logic.

And,

If you're going to do judo then you're sometimes going to get injured.
You *are* going to do judo.
Therefore you're sometimes going to get injured.

These arguments have a similar shape or structure. They are constructed in the same sort of way. In logic, the structure of an argument is called its form.

modus ponens
The two arguments we have just considered both have the form:

If [sentence *p*] is true then [sentence *q*] is true.
[Sentence *p*] is true.
Therefore [sentence *q*] is true.

Or, more succinctly:

If *p* then *q*
p
Therefore *q*

We know that arguments constructed this way must be valid, since if one statement implies another, and the first statement is true, then the second statement must also be true. Logicians label this valid form of argument *modus ponens* (Latin for "method of affirming").

At this point, it will be helpful to introduce a couple more technical terms: antecedent and consequent.

In any statement with an "if… then…" construction, the antecedent is the bit following "if" and the consequent is the bit following "then." For example, in the statement, "If John studied philosophy then he must have studied logic," the antecedent is "John studied philosophy," and the consequent is "he must have studied logic."

In *modus ponens* the antecedent gets affirmed, and this logically entails the truth of the consequent. For this reason, *modus ponens* is sometimes referred to as affirming the antecedent.

modus tollens

Here's another valid argument form:

> **If [sentence *p*] is true then [sentence *q*] is true.**
> **[Sentence *q*] is not true.**
> **Therefore [sentence *p*] is not true.**

Or, more succinctly:

> **If *p* then *q***
> **Not-*q***
> **Therefore not-*p***

This one is called *modus tollens* (Latin for "method of denying"). Any argument that takes this form is valid, since if one statement logically implies another, and the second statement is untrue, then the first statement must also be untrue. Here's an example:

> **If this were your computer, you would know the password.**
> **You don't know the password.**
> **Therefore this isn't your computer.**

In *modus tollens*, the consequent is denied, and this logically entails the nontruth of the antecedent. So *modus tollens* is sometimes referred to as denying the consequent.

hypothetical syllogism

A hypothetical syllogism is a type of deductive argument that has a conditional statement (an "if… then…" statement) for one or more of its premises.

A third type of deductively valid argument is named after the hypothetical syllogism, and has the following form:

> **If [sentence *p*] is true then [sentence *q*] is true.**
> **If [sentence *q*] is true then [sentence *r*] is true.**
> **Therefore if [sentence *p*] is true then [sentence *r*] is true.**

That is:

> **If *p* then *q***
> **If *q* then *r***
> **Therefore if *p* then *r***

For example:

**If you study hard, you will pass your exams.
If you pass your exams, you will get a pay raise.
Therefore if you study hard you will get a pay raise.**

Arguments of this type are valid, since if one thing implies a second thing, and that second thing implies a third thing, then the first thing implies the third. In fact, hypothetical syllogisms can be formed by stringing together any number of linked hypotheticals, and will remain valid. So:

**If p then q
If q then r
If r then s
If s then t
Therefore if p then t**

disjunctive syllogism

A disjunctive syllogism is a type of deductive argument that has a disjunctive statement (an "either… or…" statement) as one of its premises.

A fourth valid argument is named after the disjunctive syllogism and has the form:

**[Sentence p] is true or [sentence q] is true.
[Sentence p] is not true.
Therefore, [sentence q] is true.**

More succinctly:

**p or q
Not-p
Therefore q**

Example:

**Either she's stupid or she's a liar.
She's not stupid.
Therefore she's a liar.**

Arguments of this type are valid, since if one of two options is true, and we can be certain that one of them is false, then the other must be true.

dilemma

A fifth type of valid argument is the constructive dilemma, or simply dilemma. It has the form:

**If [sentence p] is true then [sentence q] is true.
If [sentence r] is true then [sentence s] is true.
[Sentence p] is true or [sentence r] is true.
Therefore [sentence q] is true or [sentence s] is true.**

More succinctly:

**If p then q
If r then s
p or r
Therefore q or s**

For example:

> **If it stays dry, then I'll play soccer.**
> **If it continues to rain, then I'll watch soccer on TV.**
> **Either it will stay dry or it will continue to rain.**
> **Therefore I'll either play soccer or watch it on TV.**

It is worth noting, for the sake of completeness, that there is an alternative form of the dilemma, which is known as the destructive dilemma. It looks like this:

> **If p then q**
> **If r then s**
> **Not-q or not-s**
> **Therefore not-p or not-r**

For example:

> **If he has forgotten his umbrella, he will be wet.**
> **If he has forgotten his overcoat, he will be cold.**
> **He is not wet or he is not cold.**
> **Therefore he has not forgotten his coat or he has not forgotten his umbrella.**

the inclusive and the exclusive "or"

The English word "or" is very small but very tricky, in that it can be used in two quite different senses. It can be used in an *exclusive* sense. For example, a fixed-price menu might include soup or salad, in which case you can have *either* soup *or* salad but *not both*. Alternatively, it can be used in an *inclusive* sense. So, if a restaurant's dress code informs you that you can't wear shorts or baseball caps, it means you'll be denied entry if you're wearing *either* short pants *or* a baseball cap—or *both*.

In ordinary language, you have to rely on context to decide which sense of "or" is being used. In logic, it is always used in the inclusive sense unless otherwise stated. The disjunctive syllogism and the dilemma are valid for both the inclusive and the exclusive *or*.

fallacies

We have seen that invalid arguments sometimes bear a close resemblance to valid ones. In logic, faulty types of argument with an appearance of validity are labeled **fallacies**. To the untrained eye they can be difficult to spot and can mislead the unwary into accepting conclusions for which there's insufficient or no justification.

In philosophy, it's important to be able to spot faulty reasoning. So the identification of fallacies forms an important part of the study of logic.

formal and informal fallacies

Strictly speaking, there are two kinds of fallacy:

1 **Formal fallacies** These are types of argument that are faulty because of a flaw in their logical structure. They are invalid in the technical sense of the word. That is, their premises don't logically entail their conclusions.

2 **Informal fallacies** These are types of argument that are unreliable, not so much because of a flaw in their logical structure but rather because of some other kind of error. The fault lies more with their content than with their form. For example, they may rely on a dubious implied assumption.

Formal fallacies are fallacies in the strictest sense of the word. But the word "fallacy" is also used in a looser sense to refer to any unreliable type of argument, including fallacies of the informal kind.

common fallacies

Philosophers have been identifying and labeling fallacies since the time of Aristotle, who listed 13 of them in his *De Sophisticis Elenchis* ("Sophistical Refutations"). Fallacy-collecting was a favorite pastime of medieval philosophers, too, which explains why so many of them have Latin names.

The *Internet Encyclopedia of Philosophy* currently lists 209 fallacies. Some of them have impressive-sounding Latin names, such as *ad ignorantiam*, *petitio principii*, and *argumentum consensus gentium*. Others have brash modern names, including Scare Tactic, Texas Sharpshooter, and Mob Appeal.

On the following pages, you'll find a small representative selection of fallacies of both the formal and informal varieties.

affirming the consequent

The following is a valid argument:

> **If Father Christmas doesn't exist then someone bought those presents.**
> **Father Christmas doesn't exist.**
> **So someone bought those presents.**

As the last section explained, this is an example of the valid argument form *modus ponens*, which can be expressed as follows:

> **If** p **then** q
> p
> **Therefore** q

The following argument, however, despite its apparent similarity, is invalid:

> **If Father Christmas doesn't exist then someone bought those presents.**
> **Someone bought those presents.**
> **So Father Christmas doesn't exist.**

It's invalid because it is possible for the premises to be true and yet for the conclusion to be false. That is, it's possible that, although Father Christmas does exist, those particular presents were bought by someone else.

This fallacious form of argument takes the form:

> **If** p **then** q
> q
> **Therefore** p

In the first argument (the valid one) the antecedent is affirmed, thus guaranteeing the truth of the consequent. But in the second argument (the invalid one) the consequent is affirmed, and this does not guarantee the truth of the antecedent. For this reason, this fallacy is known as affirming the consequent.

Since the fault of this fallacy lies with its logical structure it's a formal fallacy.

post hoc ergo propter hoc

Post hoc ergo propter hoc is a Latin phrase which translates as "after this, therefore on account of this." It's used to label a faulty but very common way of reasoning: the assumption that because one event preceded another it must have caused it.

Here's an example, in everyday language:

> **We prayed that the rain would stop in time for the picnic. And the rain *did* stop in time for the picnic. So our prayers were answered.**

Way back in the fourth century BCE, Aristotle observed people's tendency to fall into this flawed way of thinking and shrewdly noted: "Politicians are especially fond of taking this line. Thus Demades said that the policy of Demosthenes was the cause of all the mischief, for after it the war occurred."

The fact that two events occur consecutively doesn't necessarily mean that they're connected, even though they may appear connected in our thoughts. For example, I may take a cold remedy and then feel better the following day. But this doesn't prove that the remedy was effective, since I might have gotten better anyway.

The problem with these arguments isn't so much with their logical structure as with the underlying assumption that because two events occurred consecutively they must have been connected. So *post hoc ergo propter hoc* is an informal fallacy.

ad hominem

The *ad hominem* (Latin, meaning "to the person") fallacy is a faulty type of argument in which, quoting Aristotle, "persons direct their solutions against the man not against his arguments."

fun with fallacies

The ability to spot fallacies is as useful in everyday life as it is in philosophy. It is also tremendous fun. Once you can identify and label the most common fallacies, you'll see them cropping up all the time. You'll find yourself, whenever you read a newspaper article or listen to politician's speech or follow a debate on Facebook, saying to yourself, "*post hoc ergo propter hoc...* affirming the consequent... undistributed middle... *ad hominem...*"

Here's an example, in everyday language:

We needn't give too much credence to the economic arguments of a man who is known to have slept with prostitutes!

The *ad hominem* fallacy shifts the emphasis from the content of someone's views or arguments to some nonrelevant aspect of their character. The word "nonrelevant" is very important, since *ad hominem* arguments can be legitimate if they focus on some relevant aspect of a person's character. For example:

We needn't give too much credence to the economic arguments of a man who has had to declare himself bankrupt three times.

The fallacious form of *ad hominem* enjoys frequent use in everyday life. It's a favorite of journalists, politicians, and Facebook-ranters because it allows them to denounce other people's views and arguments without the irksome necessity of having to understand—or even listen to—them.

The *argumentum ad hominem* is an informal fallacy.

fallacy of the undistributed middle

The following argument is clearly absurd:

**All cats like milk.
My nephew likes milk.
Therefore my nephew is a cat.**

But it is, in fact, a commonly used fallacious form of argument. Here's a more realistic one:

All intellectuals wear spectacles.
Mrs. Smith wears spectacles.
Therefore Mrs. Smith is an intellectual.

And if that example seems absurd, too, bear in mind that the Khmer Rouge adopted the same pattern of reasoning to help them identify and execute large numbers of "intellectuals" in Cambodia in the 1970s.

This fallacy is labeled the undistributed middle. It's a formal fallacy with the form:

All Z is B
All Y is B
Therefore Y is Z

The fallacy acquired its name for technical reasons that needn't concern us here. It's more important to note that it's not always as easy to spot as you might think, and variations of it are often used, quite cynically, to influence opinion. We met a good example of this earlier in this chapter:

All greedy and selfish people support the Blue Party.
Helen supports the Blue Party.
Therefore Helen is greedy and selfish.

black-or-white fallacy

The black-or-white fallacy is an informal fallacy which involves the presentation of only two alternatives where, in fact, more alternatives exist. Sometimes its use is blatant, as in, "Will you accept Christ as your personal savior, or will you burn in Hell for all eternity?"

At other times, the alternatives are limited in a slightly more subtle way, as in, "So, you don't support the new law-and-order bill? Then you must favor the rights of criminals over the rights of victims." This ignores the possibility that someone who doesn't favor the rights of the criminal over the rights of the victim might nonetheless have reasons for rejecting the bill.

Exploiters of the black-or-white fallacy generally keep the structure of their arguments deliberately vague. But the hidden structure is as follows:

Either claim X is true or claim Y is true.
Claim X is not true.
Therefore claim Y is true.

Readers will recognize this as the valid argument form disjunctive syllogism. But in the black-or-white fallacy the first premise is always falsely asserted. That is, it is asserted in circumstances where claim X and claim Y might both be false.

The black-or-white fallacy is often used by Facebook-users to garner likes for their posts, as in, "Hit the 'like' button if you are against animal cruelty. Ignore if you are happy for puppies to be tortured." This ignores an important alternative—that while you are against animal cruelty, you feel no compulsion to hit a button to prove it.

Aristotle & his logic

The Greek philosopher and scientist Aristotle (384–22 BCE) is one of the undisputed giants of philosophy. He was a great polymath who had a tremendous influence upon almost every branch of knowledge he touched.

Aristotle was born in Stagira in Macedonia. He later traveled to Athens and enrolled in Plato's school of philosophy, the Academy. He was enormously talented and expected to inherit the school on Plato's death. But another student was chosen, and Aristotle opened his own school, the Lyceum.

His achievements were astonishing. He organized and classified the various sciences that we know today (physics, biology, psychology, etc.), invented the science of logic, and formulated influential theories on politics, ethics, metaphysics, aesthetics, literary criticism, and a whole lot more.

Aristotle once tutored fellow-Macedonian Alexander the Great. After Alexander's death, in 323 BCE, anti-Macedonian feeling spread throughout Athens, and Aristotle found himself on a trumped-up charge of impiety. Mindful of the fate of Socrates, he fled to Chalcis, where he died, aged 63.

Aristotle's logic

Aristotle claimed to be the founder of logic. And his claim was a perfectly valid one. Of course, before Aristotle, people had used the powers of reason to build and to assess arguments. But Aristotle was the first thinker to undertake a systematic study of argumentative reasoning; the first to construct a theory of rules of correct thought. He considered logic to be a general tool that could be used to acquire reliable knowledge in all areas of human inquiry.

His success in constructing his system was such that his ideas dominated the science of logic and formed the basis for logical studies right up until the 19th century. It's a testament to his extraordinary genius that his theory of logic, although the first of its kind, was able to hold sway for so long.

the syllogism

The core of Aristotle's logic is the syllogism, which he defined as a "discourse in which, certain things being stated, something other than what is stated follows of necessity from their being so."

Put in more familiar terms, a syllogism is a deductive argument which consists of a number of premises and a conclusion. The premises are "things being stated" and the conclusion is "something other than what is stated" which "follows of necessity" from the premises. A well-known example of the most basic form of syllogism is:

All humans are mortal.
Socrates is human.
Therefore Socrates is mortal.

In the *Prior Analytics*, one of his works on logic, Aristotle investigates the different forms the syllogism can take and identifies which of them are valid.

logic after Aristotle

Until 150 years ago, Aristotle was widely deemed to have said almost all there was to say about logic. But, in fact, his logic left a lot unsaid. It didn't, for example, deal with inferences involving propositions joined by the likes of "and," "or," and "if… then."

These limitations became clear with the rise of modern formal logic in the 19th century, a time when developments in mathematics and science led to significant innovations and advances in logic. For example: the French astronomer and mathematician Pierre-Simon Laplace propounded a logical theory of probability; the British philosopher and logician John Venn invented a system of diagrams that could be used to represent logical relationships and assess the validity of inferences; and the German mathematician and philosopher Gottleb Frege introduced a mathematical system of logical notation. These and other innovations ushered in the era of modern formal logic, which takes the ideas of philosophical logic and puts them into a mathematical framework.

schematic lettering

The use of schematic lettering to bring out the patterns of arguments was another of Aristotle's inventions. For example, representing

All humans are mortal.
Socrates is a human.
Therefore Socrates is mortal.

by

All H are M.
S is H.
Therefore S is M.

This incredibly useful technique is still widely used by philosophers today. In fact, it is an essential tool in the study of logic and inference, as the example arguments in the previous sections of this chapter demonstrate.

paradoxes

So far, logic has been represented as a powerful and dependable tool for determining whether arguments are good or bad. Logic is indeed such a tool. But what if it were to oppose itself? What if apparently impeccable reasoning were able to demonstrate the soundness of arguments with contradictory conclusions? Situations of this nature are of intense interest to philosophers.

In philosophy, an argument that appears to generate contradictory conclusions is known as a paradox. Every paradox represents a challenge to the philosopher to identify the false step, the error in reasoning, linguistic ambiguity, or the incorrect assumption that appears to set logic against itself.

Philosophers have been identifying, collecting, labeling, discussing, and attempting to resolve paradoxes ever since philosophy began. Over time, many have been resolved. But others have proven very tough nuts to crack and are still being debated today.

Galileo's paradox

In the previous paragraph, a paradox was defined as an argument that appears to generate contradictory conclusions. It would be helpful, before going any further, to flesh this definition out a little.

In his 1988 book *Paradoxes*, the contemporary philosopher R. M. Sainsbury gives what I believe is a very full, clear, and helpful definition. He says that a paradox is "an unacceptable conclusion derived by seemingly unassailable reasoning from apparently uncontroversial premises."

To illustrate this, here's a very famous paradox from the great Italian scientist, Galileo Galilei (1564–1642). In 1638, in his *Dialogues Concerning Two New Sciences*, Galileo demonstrated that there are fewer square numbers than there are natural numbers. You can confirm this for yourself just by looking:

NATURAL NUMBERS	1 2 3 4 5 6 7 8 9 10 11 12 13 14 15 16...
SQUARE NUMBERS	1 4 9 16...

Clearly, the natural numbers outnumber the square numbers. At the same time, Galileo demonstrated that there are just as many square numbers as there are

don't think ill of the paradox

Your attitude toward paradoxes can reveal a lot about your aptitude for philosophy.

I can illustrate this with a personal anecdote. Once, while socializing with three friends, I somehow found myself telling them about the two-envelope paradox (see pages 50–1). Their reactions were revealing. The first friend didn't really follow the logic of the argument and quickly lost interest. The second understood the argument perfectly well but dismissed it with a shrug of the shoulders and the words, "Yeah, that's weird!" The third spent the rest of the evening fretting about it and trying to find some way to resolve it.

None of them had studied philosophy, but to me it seemed clear that the third one had both the temperament and the aptitude for it. Philosophers are curious creatures. They hanker after knowledge and certainty. But, at the same time, they are drawn to those questions that are most shrouded in perplexity and doubt.

The Danish philosopher Søren Kierkegaard (1813–1855) put it beautifully:

But one must not think ill of the paradox, for the paradox is the passion of thought, and the thinker without the paradox is like the lover without passion: a mediocre fellow. But the ultimate potentiation of every passion is always to will its own downfall, and so it is also the ultimate passion of the understanding to will the collision, although in one way or another the collision must become its downfall. This, then, is the ultimate paradox of thought: to want to discover something that thought itself cannot think.

pick an envelope

This fascinating paradox was devised by the German mathematician Edmund Landau (1877–1938). Imagine you are presented with two sealed envelopes containing cash, and you are told that one of them contains twice as much as the other. You are invited to pick one and keep the contents. You make your choice, but before you open the envelope you are given the chance to change your mind. What should you do?

Clearly *there's no advantage in swapping*. You made a random choice between two envelopes. So there's an evens chance that you've already chosen the one with the most money. If you swap for the other envelope, your chances will still be evens. So what's the point?

But, then again, a little reflection shows that *there is an advantage in swapping*. The envelope you have chosen contains a certain amount, say 1,000 dollars. If you make an unlucky swap to the lower-value envelope, it will contain just 500 dollars. So you'll be 500 dollars worse off. But if you make a lucky swap to the higher-value envelope, you'll get 2,000 dollars, which will make you 1,000 dollars better off. This means that swapping gives you an evens chance of losing a mere 500 dollars and an evens chance of gaining a whopping 1,000 dollars. So clearly you should swap.

More generally (for the mathematicians among you), if your original envelope contains x dollars you'll either make a bad swap and get 0.5x dollars or you'll make a good swap and get 2x dollars. So swapping has an expected value of ($\frac{1}{2}$ x 0.5x) + ($\frac{1}{2}$ x 2x) = 1.25x dollars. That's an expected gain of 25%. Clearly, then, you ought to swap.

Once again, we have contradictory conclusions—there's no advantage in swapping; there's an advantage in swapping—derived from apparently impeccable reasoning.

natural numbers. Again, you can confirm this for yourself just by looking:

NATURAL NUMBERS	1	2	3	4	5	6	7	8	9	10...
SQUARE NUMBERS	1	4	9	16	25	36	49	64	81	100...

Clearly, there is a square number for every natural number. So here we have contradictory conclusions—there are fewer square numbers than naturals; there are just as many square numbers as naturals—supported by apparently valid reasoning. *That's* a paradox.

This sort of thing really shouldn't happen. It shouldn't be possible to prove two things that are contradictory.

Galileo tried to resolve the paradox by saying that since the list of natural numbers and the list of square numbers are infinite, it's inappropriate even to try to compare their sizes. Using such terms as "fewer than" and "just as many" in this context simply doesn't make sense.

But the paradox wasn't properly resolved until 300 years later when the German mathematician Georg Cantor (1845–1918) found a way of comparing the sizes of infinite sets and demonstrated that the set of square numbers is the same size as the set of natural numbers.

the two-envelope paradox

My personal favorite is the two-envelope paradox, described opposite. Read it through and then challenge yourself to find the false premise or logical misstep hidden somewhere in this apparently impeccable chain of reasoning.

This is a problem that philosophers can't ignore, because if contradictory conclusions really *can* be derived from true premises using sound reasoning then logic implodes In fact, although progress has been made on the two-envelope paradox, it is debatable whether it has yet been fully resolved.

the liar paradox

Some of the most complex and intractable paradoxes can be very simply stated. A prime example is the liar paradox. This was devised by the ancient Greek philosopher Eubulides of Miletus, a contemporary of Aristotle, who expressed it in the form of a riddle: "A man says that he is lying. Is what he says true or false?"

This is the kind of puzzle that can send your logic circuits into meltdown, since a moment's reflection reveals that if what he says is true then it is false; whereas if what he says is false then it is true. There are a lots of variations on the liar paradox. The simplest, and most difficult, is: "This statement is false." Once again, if the statement is true then it is false; whereas if it is false then it is true.

This tiny little statement has had philosophers, logicians, linguists, and mathematicians straining their brains for the last 2,500 years and is one of the most important paradoxes ever devised. The next section explains why.

true or false?

"This statement is false." At first sight, this sentence, the most simple version of the liar paradox, looks like a mere riddle, but, in fact, it challenges our most basic assumptions about logic and thought.

Consider the following propositions:

All men are mortal.
The moon's a balloon.
There's life on other planets.

Clearly, the first one's true whereas the second one's false. But what about the third? Well, no one knows for sure whether there's life on other planets, so no one knows whether it's true or false. What we do know, however, is that it's either true or false and not both.

The same holds true for all propositions. They're true or else they're false, and there is no other option.

It's possible, of course, to construct any number of sentences that are neither true nor false. Examples include:

Goodbye.
Don't forget to write!
Who were you talking to last night?

But these are not propositions. They're not statements we can argue about, believe, or disbelieve, so they don't concern us here.

Aristotle revisited

Aristotle identified two principles of logic and thought that encapsulate the reasoning above: the law of the excluded middle and the law of contradiction.

The law of the excluded middle states that "there is nothing between asserting and denying." In other words, every proposition is true or false and there's no middle ground. The law of contradiction states that a proposition cannot be both true and, at the same time, false.

Taken together, these two laws require that every proposition is either true or false but not both. These principles are so basic that if we don't presume their soundness we seem unable to reason at all.

To see that this is so, imagine that someone were to deny the law of contradiction. In that case, any statement they made would be meaningless. For instance, if they declared that "an apple is a fruit" they would not thereby exclude the possibility that an apple is not a fruit. And if they claimed that "the law of contradiction is unsound" they would not thereby exclude the possibility that the law of contradiction is sound.

Anyone seeking to deny the law of the excluded middle would encounter similar difficulties. Thus, if someone were to claim "the law of the excluded middle is not true," it would not thereby follow that the law of the excluded middle is false.

Any attempt at reasoning seems to presuppose the soundness of both laws. Clearly, principles so basic cannot allow any exceptions. Or can they?

true, false, both, or neither?

Consider the following propositions:

This statement is false.
This statement is true.

Let's begin with "this statement is false," the familiar liar paradox. Is it true or false? Well, if it's true then it's false, whereas if it's false then it's true. But, in that case, we seem to have a proposition that breaks the law of contradiction. It appears to be both true and, at the same time, false.

Now consider the second statement, "this statement is true." This is a kind of cousin to the liar paradox. Is it true or false? Well, if it's true then what it says is true whereas if it's false then what it says is false. Both assumptions are perfectly consistent, and there's no way of determining the issue one way or the other.

But, in that case, we seem to have a proposition that breaks the law of the excluded middle. It appears to be neither true nor false. These two innocuous-looking propositions thus present a challenge to our most basic assumptions about logic and thought.

responses

The liar paradox has provided philosophers with food for thought since ancient times, and still there's no agreed solution. One possible solution is to deny that propositions such as "this statement is false" are meaningful. But this is unsatisfactory unless we can state precisely *why* they're not meaningful. Another possible solution is to accept that a proposition such as "this statement is false" really is both true and, at the same time, false. But this requires a rejection of classical logic.

Needless to say, the rejection of classical logic is a very radical step to take—and yet, a number of philosophers, notably Professor Graham Priest, have taken it. They have championed a new kind of logic, known as paraconsistent logic, which denies, among other things, the legitimacy of the law of contradiction. In paraconsistent logic, propositions can be both true and, at the same time, false.

The sky is blue.
The sky is not blue.
Therefore Ringo was the most creative
Beatle.

ex falso quodlibet

Many readers will protest that whatever
medieval logicians might say, *ex falso
quodlibet*—roughly "from falsehood,
anything follows"—is a load of bunk.
Tomatoes are one thing, and David
Beckham's butt is another. So how can we
argue from one to the other? Let's find out.

some background

Before demonstrating the validity of the
principle of explosion we need to do a bit
of spadework. First, consider the statement
"John is sad or Alan is hungry." This is
comprised of two clauses linked by or. In
classical logic, statements like this are true
provided that one or both of the constituent
clauses is true. This means that if "John
is sad" is true then "John is sad or Alan is
hungry" is also true.

Next, consider the statement "Mary is
sleepy or Sarah is noisy." If this statement is
true but "Mary is sleepy" is false then clearly
"Sarah is noisy" must be true.

the principle of explosion

Armed with this information, let's re-
examine the David Beckham argument.
We'll begin with the premises:

    1. A tomato is a fruit.

the principle of explosion

Logicians have long appreciated that
contradictory premises entail any
conclusion. In medieval times this
startling but valid rule of inference
was known as *ex falso quodlibet*.
Nowadays it is often labeled the
principle of explosion.

Consider the following argument:

    A tomato is a fruit.
    A tomato is not a fruit.
    **Therefore David Beckham has a pimple
    on his butt.**

Contrary to appearances, it's perfectly
valid. Given that a tomato both is and is
not a fruit, we can validly infer that David
Beckham has a pimple on his butt. In fact,
given contradictory premises we can validly
infer just about anything. As follows:

2. A tomato is not a fruit.

Now, if it's true that "a tomato is a fruit" then "a tomato is a fruit or David Beckham has a pimple on his butt" is also true. So, now we can say:

1. A tomato is a fruit.
2. A tomato is not a fruit.
3. A tomato is a fruit or David Beckham has a pimple on his butt (from 1.).

But if it's true that "a tomato is a fruit or David Beckham has a pimple on his butt" and also true that "a tomato is not a fruit" then it must be true that "David Beckham has a pimple on his butt." So:

1. A tomato is a fruit.
2. A tomato is not a fruit.
3. A tomato is a fruit or David Beckham has a pimple on his butt (from 1).
4. David Beckham has a pimple on his butt (from 2 and 3).

To make the logical structure of the argument clearer, if P stands for "a tomato is a fruit" and Q for "David Beckham has a pimple on his butt," we have:

1. P is true
2. P is false
3. P is true or Q is true (from 1)
4. Q is true (from 2 and 3)

P and Q could stand for any proposition, so

I am the pope

According to one old story, the English mathematician and philosopher A. N. Whitehead was once challenged to demonstrate that it is possible to prove anything using contradictory premises. "Starting from the premise that four equals three, prove that you are the pope," he was asked.

"Easy!" Whitehead replied. "Four equals three. Subtract two from each side, then two equals one. It is commonly known that the pope and I are two people. Therefore the pope and I are one." (Some versions of the story substitute J. M. E. McTaggart, G. H. Hardy, or Bertrand Russell for Whitehead. But never mind. It's a great story anyway.)

this is a general proof that anything can be inferred from contradictory premises.

valid but not sound

The principle of explosion is a perfectly good rule of inference according to classical logic. You really *can* derive anything from contradictory premises. But we have to remember that *ex falso quodlibet* arguments, while valid, are not sound. Classical logicians hold that contradictions are never true, meaning that one of the premises must always be false, so we can't use the principle of explosion to actually prove anything.

chapter three

what is epistemology?

knowledge
& belief

Epistemology is the branch of philosophy concerned with the nature and scope of human knowledge. It asks questions such as "What is knowledge?" and "What can we know?" and "How can we know it?" The word derives from the Greek word *episteme*, which means "knowledge."

The desire to know, rather than merely to believe, has been a key motivation for many philosophers. Socrates and Descartes were two intellectual giants consumed by that desire. Socrates believed that right actions depend on right opinions; once we truly know and understand what is good we will most certainly do it. That's why he sought, using his method of elenchus, to gain reliable knowledge of ethical matters. He saw knowledge as the key to a good, well-lived life and valued it accordingly.

Descartes, although his motivations were different, was just as dedicated to the pursuit of knowledge. He had noted with dismay how many errors had been made in philosophy and the sciences by earlier thinkers and how many false beliefs he had accepted as true on their authority. This realization inspired his own bold and brilliant attempt to clear away the errors of the past and to establish philosophy and the sciences anew on the unshakable foundations of secure knowledge.

knowledge versus belief

Knowledge has always held a particular fascination for philosophers. But what exactly is it? How does knowledge differ from mere belief?

Generally speaking, philosophers tend not to think of knowledge and belief as entirely different things. They tend to regard knowing as a special kind of believing. Or, put slightly differently, they consider knowledge to be a subset of belief.

We all have numerous beliefs. Some of these beliefs count as knowledge and some of them don't. We can believe things without knowing them, but we can't know things without believing them. But what is it that sets apart the things we know from the rest of our beliefs? What are the distinguishing features of knowledge?

truth

The first criterion that sets these things apart is truth. Only true beliefs can count

what is truth?

Pontius Pilate famously asked Jesus, "What is truth?" This is a thorny question, which philosophers have been debating since before the time of Christ and are still debating.

One answer that has a lot of intuitive plausibility is that what we say or believe is true if it corresponds to the way things actually are—to the facts. Aristotle expressed this view, in his own inimitable fashion, in the *Metaphysics*. He wrote: "To say of what is that it is not, or of what is not that it is, is false, while to say of what is that it is, and of what is not that it is not, is true."

The medieval philosopher and Roman Catholic saint, Thomas Aquinas (1225–74), put it rather more simply when he wrote: "A judgment is said to be true when it conforms to the external reality." In modern philosophy this is known as the correspondence theory of truth. At the heart of this theory is the notion that the world contains facts, which, in the words of Bertrand Russell, "are what they are whatever we may choose to think about them."

Our beliefs have reference to these facts, and with reference to these facts are either true or false. So, for example, the belief that the cat is on the mat is true if, and only if, it is a fact that the world contains *the cat* and *the mat* and that the former is in contact with and supported by the latter.

The correspondence theory of truth is by no means uncontroversial. There are a number of competing theories such as the coherence theory, the constructivist theory, the consensus theory, and the pragmatic theory. But to keep things simple we'll stick with the intuitively plausible correspondence theory and consider truth to be a matter of statements and beliefs conforming, somehow, to facts.

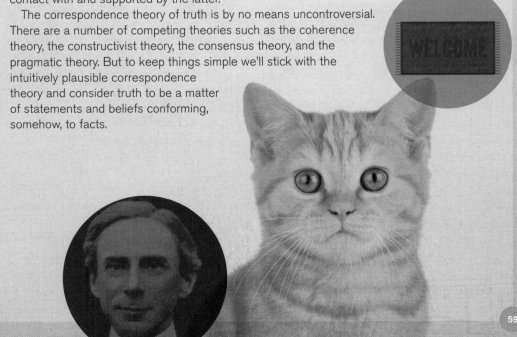

types of knowledge

We can use the word "know" in a number of different ways. For example, I can say that I *know* how to peel a banana; that I *know* Clarinda's Tearoom in Edinburgh; and that I *know* that Jupiter is larger than Venus.

Knowing how to peel a banana is an example of what is sometimes called ability knowledge. Knowing Clarinda's Tearoom in Edinburgh is an example of what is sometimes called acquaintance knowledge. And knowing that Jupiter is larger than Venus is an example of what philosophers call propositional knowledge.

A proposition is a declarative statement, a statement that declares that something is or is not the case. So, propositional knowledge is essentially knowledge of facts, knowledge that certain things are or are not the case.

Epistemologists are interested in all three kinds of knowledge, but especially interested in propositional knowledge. Propositional knowledge is the most sophisticated kind of knowledge. An ape can have ability knowledge by knowing how to peel a banana; and an ape could acquire acquaintance knowledge of Clarinda's Tearoom; but an ape would seem to be incapable of acquiring propositional knowledge, except perhaps of an exceedingly rudimentary kind.

as knowledge. It's possible to believe something that isn't true, but it isn't possible to know something that isn't true. For example, I might believe that Charles Dickens wrote *Pride and Prejudice*, but I can't know that he wrote it, because he didn't. I may feel supremely confident in my belief. I may feel quite certain that I know it. But I don't know it, and I can't know it, because it isn't true. Only true beliefs can count as knowledge.

justification

The second criterion is justification. I may firmly believe something—and it may happen to be true—but if I don't have sufficient justification for believing it then I don't really know it.

Plato gives an example of this in the *Theaetetus*, a dialogue in which Socrates discusses the nature of knowledge with a talented young geometry student. At one point, Theaetetus suggests that knowledge is "true judgment," but Socrates objects that true judgments don't necessarily count as knowledge. He points out that a clever lawyer may, by the wiles of his craft, convince a jury of an opinion which is, in fact, true but for which there isn't really any proper evidence. In this case, although the members of the jury make a true judgment, they don't have knowledge.

Here's another example. A woman sitting at a roulette table may, after observing the ball land on red five times in a row, feel convinced that it must land on black on the next spin of the wheel. Her belief may turn out to be a true one, since the ball may indeed land on black. But her belief doesn't count as knowledge as it was founded on incorrect reasoning.

So, to count as knowledge a belief must not only be true, it must also be justified. It must be based on proper evidence and sound reasoning.

justified true belief (JTB)

Summing up, we know something if: a) we believe it; b) it is true; and c) we are justified in believing it. Or, putting it even more succinctly, knowledge is justified true belief.

This is known as the tripartite theory of knowledge, or, more snappily, as the JTB theory. It can be traced all the way back to Plato, and, although it suffered a bruising at the hands of the American philosopher Edmund L. Gettier in the early 1960s (see page 68), it still serves quite well as a working definition of knowledge.

According to the tripartite theory, belief, truth, and justification are necessary and sufficient conditions for knowledge. *Necessary* because unless all three conditions are met you don't have knowledge, and *sufficient* because when all three conditions are met nothing more is required.

what counts as justification?

We will consider Gettier's objections to the JTB theory shortly. But, for the present, we will work on the assumption that knowledge is justified true belief. Here, an important question arises. How much justification does a true belief require in order for it to count as knowledge? Clearly, justification is a matter of degree. We are justified to an overwhelming degree in believing some things but justified to a lesser degree in believing others.

For example, I believe that three sevens are 21. Is this belief justified? Yes. I have compelling reasons for believing it. It's one of the facts I committed to memory when I learned my multiplication tables as a child. I can check it by counting in sevens on my fingers. And my calculator agrees, too. With such a weight of evidence, I seem entirely justified in claiming not merely to believe but to know that three sevens are 21.

I also believe that Charles Dickens wrote *A Christmas Carol*. As a lifelong reader and admirer of Dickens, I'm absolutely certain of this. I own the book. I've read it more than once. I've read numerous accounts of how Dickens came to write it. And Google agrees. Once again, I can claim knowledge of it.

I also believe that my wife is in a hair salon in the Harajuku district of Tokyo right now. Am I justified in believing it? Yes. She told me this morning that that's where she was going, and she texted me ten minutes ago to say she's arrived. Is my justification for this belief as well-founded as the others? Well, no. She may have popped out for some reason; they may have had a fire alarm at the salon and had to evacuate the building; she may have lied to me about her whereabouts. So, although my belief is justified, the degree of justification isn't overwhelming. Can I claim, then, to *know* that she is in a hair salon in Harajuku? I would say not. This suggests that among my numerous beliefs, the only ones that really count as knowledge are those for which there is overwhelming evidence, for which there is little or no possibility of error. But is it realistic to use such a stringent standard of justification? Wouldn't that severely limit the number of things that I can claim to know?

infallibilism

Some philosophers have taken the view that in order to have knowledge you must have a belief which is infallible. That is, you must have a belief that couldn't possibly be in error. This view goes by the name of "infallibilism."

Infallibilism has a lot of intuitive appeal. My hair-salon example demonstrates that most of us are willing to admit that if a belief admits of even a small degree of doubt then it doesn't really count as knowledge. Infallibilists merely push this idea to its natural conclusion. They claim that if any doubt, however slight or far-fetched, can be raised against a belief then it doesn't strictly count as knowledge.

This sounds reasonable. But it opens up a whole epistemological can of worms. Because once you restrict knowledge to those beliefs about which you can't possibly be mistaken, you quickly discover that there's little, if anything, that you really know.

a personal note...

The desire to replace belief with knowledge was the starting point of my own philosophical quest.

From childhood, I had been taught to believe the teachings of a certain fundamentalist Christian sect. But as I grew into adulthood I began to worry that perhaps I had acquired those beliefs without proper justification.

I knew very little about philosophy at the time. But, from what little I knew, I felt that it might offer me some intellectual tools for re-evaluating my beliefs.

As luck would have it, one of the first works I stumbled upon was Descartes's *Meditations on First Philosophy*.

From the opening lines—"Some years ago I noticed how many false things I had accepted as true in my childhood, and how doubtful were the things that I subsequently built upon them..."—I was hooked.

the method of doubt

If we were to take the infallibilist view that a belief only counts as knowledge if it can't possibly be in error, then how severely would that limit our claims to knowledge? How much of what we think we know is completely immune to doubt?

This experiment in thought was famously conducted by Descartes. He adopted what has become known as the method of doubt: a systematic procedure of rejecting, as if false, all beliefs for which there is the slightest possibility of error. His method consisted of three stages, each more radical than the last, and is recorded in his hugely influential work *Meditations on First Philosophy*.

unreliability of the senses
The first stage of the method of doubt was to reject as unreliable the evidence of the senses. In the first chapter of the *Meditations*, Descartes writes:

> **Whatever I have up till now accepted as most true and assured I have gotten either from the senses or through the senses. But from time to time I have found that the senses deceive, and it is prudent never to trust completely those who have deceived us even once.**

He gives a number of examples of how the senses can deceive us. For example, a straight stick appears bent when it is dipped into water, and a square tower can appear round when seen from a distance.

But, even though the senses aren't entirely trustworthy, surely we can trust them about some things. Surely they justify me in believing that I'm currently seated at a table, typing on my laptop. The senses might not represent the table to me entirely accurately—in fact, we can be fairly certain that they don't (see pages 16–17)—but surely they justify me in believing that the table exists and that I'm sitting at it right now.

the dream hypothesis
The second stage of Descartes's method of doubt was to call to mind the fact that even those things that seem most real and present to us might be nothing more than the stuff of dreams. As he ponders the unreliability of his senses, Descartes initially feels that he can trust them at least far enough to be

why doubt?

The *Meditations* is one of the most influential works in the entire history of philosophy. It is also required reading for every new philosophy student. One of the reasons why students are introduced to the *Meditations* early in their studies is that it is such a short, profound, and yet accessible read. Another reason—perhaps the principal reason—is the method of doubt.

Why is that? What's the big deal about doubt? Well, for Descartes, systematic doubt was a way of clearing away the clutter of false and dubious opinions so that he could make a fresh start on the business of acquiring knowledge. He likened the philosophy and science of his day to a dilapidated old building, tottering on rotten foundations. When you have a building like that, it's useless trying to shore it up or paper over the cracks. You have to tear it down and start again from scratch. This process of tearing down and starting from scratch is very useful to students of philosophy.

Philosophy is about getting to the heart of things, questioning things, challenging preconceived ideas, and using the intellect to see past the obvious. And Descartes's method of doubt is a splendid tool for doing precisely that. The point of the method isn't to get us to take seriously the notion that our lives might be a dream, still less that everything we experience and think might be delusions foisted upon us by an evil genius, rather the point is to get us to lay aside our preconceptions, reassess the way we interpret our sensory experiences, and question our habitual ways of thinking.

Descartes, through his method of doubt, forces us to reassess and revise our most basic assumptions about the world and the way we understand it.

And that, gentle reader, is where philosophy begins.

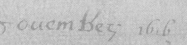

sure that he is sitting beside the fire in his bathrobe. But further reflection throws even that into doubt.

He writes:

I cannot forget that, at other times, I have been deceived in sleep by similar illusions; and, attentively considering those cases, I perceive so clearly that there exist no certain marks by which the state of waking can ever be distinguished from sleep, that I feel greatly astonished; and in amazement I almost persuade myself that I am now dreaming.

The Chinese philosopher Chuang Tzu (ca. 369 BCE–ca. 286 BCE) once said something similar. He recounts how, on one occasion, he dreamed he was a butterfly, and, upon waking, could no longer be sure if he was a man who had dreamed of being a butterfly or if he was a butterfly who was dreaming of being a man. The point is, how can we be sure that our present experiences, or even the sum total of our lives' experiences, are not the product of mere dreams or hallucinations? Perhaps we can't. But even so, aren't there still some things we can be sure of?

For instance, even if I'm dreaming right now, and even if the table I'm sitting at and the laptop I'm typing on have no real existence, can't I at least be sure that there are such things as tables and laptops? Otherwise, where do I get those ideas from? And even if tables and laptops are merely products of my imagination and exist only in my dreams, can't I at least be sure that the basic elements from which they are composed, such as colors and shapes, exist? And even if all of *that* might possibly be doubted, can't I at least be sure, whether I'm dreaming or not, that two plus three makes five and that the shape I call a square has four sides?

the evil genius

This is where the third and final stage of the method of doubt comes into play. Descartes imagines that everything he sees, hears, feels, touches, and tastes has no basis in reality but is a delusion foisted upon him by some godlike but malevolent being:

I will suppose… an evil genius, as clever and deceitful as he is powerful, who has directed his entire effort to misleading me, I will regard the heavens, the air, the earth, colors, shapes, sounds, and all external things as nothing but the deceptive games of my dreams, with which he lays a snare for my credulity.

Descartes supposes that this evil genius is so powerful and cunning that he can even manipulate his thoughts, so that he makes mistakes even when adding two and three, or when counting the sides of a square.

One wonders whether there can be any item of knowledge that is secure even against such all-encompassing doubt.

the cogito

As we learned in chapter 1, Descartes *did* find something. He realized that even if his entire life were a dream or a delusion, and even if his patterns of thinking were deeply flawed, one thing remained certain: the fact of his own existence. Even if all of his experiences were delusory, he existed. Even if his patterns of thinking were flawed, he existed. The very fact that he could think, or doubt, or even be deceived, confirmed that he existed.

He writes:

> So, after considering everything very thoroughly, I must finally conclude that the proposition, I am, I exist, is necessarily true whenever it is put forward by me or conceived in my mind.

In his 1644 work *Principles of Philosophy*, he sums up this famous insight using the Latin phrase, *cogito ergo sum* ("I think, therefore I am"). Philosophers often refer to this simply as the "cogito."

false awakenings

I remember sleeping alone once when my wife was away working, and waking in the night to discover three vampire women standing at the foot of my bed, whispering to one another and casting wicked, greedy glances my way. I realized that it was a dream, brought on, no doubt, by some uneasiness at sleeping alone and by recollections of the erotically charged scene in *Dracula* where Jonathan Harker wakes to find himself surrounded by three seductive vampire sisters. But, dream or not, the creatures looked and sounded perfectly real. It was only my intellect, as opposed to my senses, that convinced me I was only dreaming.

Fortunately, I have the ability to wake myself from nightmares, which I promptly did. I lay for a moment, heart pounding, yet relieved to be back in the real world, when suddenly I became aware that something wasn't right. I looked up to discover three vampire women standing at the foot of my bed, whispering to one another and casting wicked, greedy glances my way…

This happened three or four times, and each time it was only my intellect that convinced me that what I was seeing and hearing wasn't real, that I was having a false awakening.

Gettier problems

In 1963, the American philosopher Edmund L. Gettier published a short article which dealt a huge blow to the tripartite theory of knowledge. It demonstrated, to the satisfaction of many epistemologists, that there is more to knowledge than justified true belief.

Gettier's strategy was to provide counterexamples to the tripartite analysis. That is, to point to situations in which it would be possible to have a justified true belief which would not count as knowledge. The counterexamples he used weren't perhaps the simplest and clearest he might have chosen. So here is a simpler one that illustrates his point just as well.

Imagine that Sue wakes up one morning and looks at her trusty bedside clock. It tells her that the time is 6:25. And, in fact, the time *is* 6:25. So Sue has a belief that is both true and justified. However, unbeknown to her, one of the springs in her trusty old bedside clock broke twelve hours earlier, and the hands haven't moved since then. So it's pure luck that her belief happens to be true. Had she woken up a minute earlier or a minute later, she would have had precisely the same justification for holding a false belief.

Her belief, although true and justified, doesn't seem to count as knowledge, since it's only true through chance, through a lucky combination of circumstances. This being the case, it would seem that there must be more to knowledge than JTB.

It's possible to construct any number of such counterexamples. All you have to do is conjure up a scenario in which someone is justified in believing something that happens to be true, but that is true not for the reasons they think it is but only through happenchance. Such scenarios are known as Gettier cases or Gettier problems.

Another well-known Gettier case, originally devised by the American philosopher R. M. Chisholm (1916–99), runs along the following lines. Imagine you look into a field and see something that looks just like a sheep. Accordingly you form the justified belief that there's

Gettier's amazing paper

The story of how Edmund Gettier came to write his seminal paper on justified true belief has acquired almost legendary status in philosophical circles.

Back in the early 1960s, Gettier was an ambitious youngish philosopher who was keen to get something published in one of the respected philosophy journals. Accordingly, he looked around for a suitable subject to write about. He wasn't especially interested in epistemology, but he figured that he could quickly put together something interesting and publishable criticizing the tripartite analysis of knowledge. His resulting article, "Is Justified True Belief Knowledge?" was published in the academic journal of philosophy *Analysis* in 1963.

The article generated a lot of interest, boosted his reputation, and got him tenure at his university. Strangely, though, Gettier showed little or no interest in the debate his article stirred up and never wrote any more about it—or, indeed, about any other epistemological topic.

foundationalism and coherentism

By now it will be apparent to all readers that justifying a belief—any belief—can be a tricky business. The big difficulty with justification is that in order to justify one belief it seems necessary to refer to other beliefs. But those other beliefs also require justification by yet more beliefs. And where does it all end?

Here's an example. I believe that Charles Dickens wrote *A Christmas Carol*. I can justify this by pointing to his name on my copy of the book or by referring to various books and articles about Dickens' life and works. But what justifies me in believing that Dickens really wrote all the books that bear his name? And what justifies me in believing that I can trust the information I find in the various books and articles about him? To do so I would have to refer to further beliefs. I might justify my belief in the reliability of various articles and books by pointing out that they were written by experts who have access to trustworthy historical documents. But to justify *that* belief, I would have to refer to yet more beliefs.

This seems unsatisfactory. Unless these beliefs are eventually grounded upon a firm foundation my entire belief-system seems in danger of collapse. So *is* there an ultimate grounding for our beliefs? Some philosophers say yes, taking the view that all knowledge ultimately rests upon a foundation of basic beliefs—that is, beliefs which we know immediately to be true without having to infer them from other beliefs and which therefore require no further justification. These might include, "I feel a pain, right now," "I seem to see something blue," "Two and three make five," and "I exist." This epistemological viewpoint goes by the name "foundationalism." Foundationalists argue that without such basic beliefs we would be in a position where every belief needs to be justified by further beliefs, and so on, and so on, in an infinite and vicious regress.

Other philosophers reject this view. They claim that there *are* no basic beliefs and that all beliefs must therefore be justified by other beliefs. Furthermore, they claim that this is OK, that our nonbasic beliefs don't need to rest on basic beliefs but can instead provide mutual support for one another. By this account, we shouldn't think of knowledge as a structure grounded upon a solid foundation but instead should think of it as a web or network of interconnected beliefs.

In this case, beliefs are justified provided that they fit neatly into our overall belief-structure. That is, that they cohere with our other beliefs. This epistemological viewpoint is known as "coherentism."

a sheep in the field. In fact, what you are looking at isn't a sheep but a dog disguised as a sheep. Nonetheless, your belief is true, since there just happens to be a real sheep standing out of sight behind the dog. So you have a belief that is true and justified. But it seems wrong to claim that you have knowledge since your belief is true through a mere fluke.

responses to Gettier

Gettier problems are a real challenge to the JTB theory of knowledge. But can the theory be salvaged? Are there any satisfactory responses? One possible response is to take an infallibilist view of justification. That is, to insist that a belief only counts as knowledge if it is justified to such a degree that it couldn't possibly be mistaken.

Clearly, in the examples above, as in all Gettier cases, the true beliefs are formed in such a way that they are not infallibly justified. So, by the infallibilist account, they don't count as knowledge. The problem with this response is that it throws the baby out with the bathwater. It saves the JTB theory, but only by discounting almost everything—if not absolutely everything—that we normally count as knowledge.

Another possible response to Gettier problems is to eliminate the element of luck. That is, to insist that in order to count as knowledge a justified belief must be true not by accident but in a way that is suitably related to its means of justification. The

problem with this response is that if we seek to eliminate every trace of luck from our means of justification then we seem to get drawn back into the infallibilist position.

For example, I have a justified belief that I'm typing on my laptop right now. But my means of justification takes for granted that I'm "lucky" enough not to be dreaming, or hallucinating, or living in The Matrix, or being deceived by an evil genius.

Perhaps, though, the problem with Gettier cases isn't that they involve luck, but rather that they involve *too much* luck. Perhaps knowledge requires only that *not too much* chance or sheer fluke enters into true justified belief. But in this case, how much luck is too much luck?

JTB not enough

Most philosophers agree that Gettier succeeded in demonstrating that the tripartite theory doesn't fully capture what knowledge is, that there must be something more to knowledge than justified true belief. But there is no agreement about what that something more is. Many epistemologists have attempted to provide a more robust Gettier-proof theory of knowledge, but so far without success. The debate continues.

knowledge & experience

In epistemology, an important distinction is often made between two different kinds of knowledge: *a priori* and *a posteriori*. *A priori* knowledge is knowledge that can be gained or tested through reason alone, independently from sensory experience. This contrasts with *a posteriori* knowledge, which is dependent upon sensory experience.

We can know *a priori* that the proposition "all bachelors are unmarried" is true. We don't need to check up on the marital status of all the bachelors we can find to confirm it. Provided that we understand the meanings of the words "bachelor" and "unmarried," we understand that it must be true. Needless to say, we require sensory experience to learn these words, but *a priori* knowledge of propositions can be gained and tested independently from any experience apart from that required to learn the language in which those propositions are expressed.

As well as truths of meaning, we can also know truths of logic and mathematics a priori. So we can know that nothing can be wholly red and wholly green at the same time and that two plus three makes five.

knowledge *a posteriori*

But we can't know *a priori* that zebras sleep standing up. We can only know this by investigating the world with our senses, by observing zebras, or reading about them, or asking people about them. So the fact that zebras can sleep standing up is something we can only know *a posteriori*.

It can be helpful to think of *a priori* knowledge as the kind you can acquire simply by sitting in your chair and cogitating and *a posteriori* knowledge as the kind that requires you to get up out of your chair and investigate the world.

analytic and synthetic

As well as making a distinction between two kinds of knowledge, *a priori* and *a posteriori*, philosophers also make a distinction between two kinds of proposition: analytic and synthetic.

Analytic propositions are those which are true by definition. Here are some examples:

- **All bachelors are unmarried.**
- **A dog is an animal.**
- **A hexagon has twice as many sides as a triangle.**

Propositions such as these are true simply as a matter of language and logic. The good thing about analytic propositions, in epistemological terms, is that we can know for certain that they are true. The bad thing about them is that they provide us with no substantive information about the world. So an extraterrestrial who understood the English language but had no empirical data about our world could know that the analytic proposition "all bachelors are unmarried" must be true but would not know whether any bachelors or people actually exist in our world.

On the other hand, synthetic propositions are ones that are not true merely by definition. They make statements of fact about the world that go beyond language and logic. For example:

- **Paris is the capital city of France.**
- **Pandas eat mostly watermelon.**
- **My watch is broken.**

The good thing about synthetic propositions, in epistemological terms, is that they tell us something substantive about the world outside our minds. The bad thing about them is that they may not, in fact, be true.

what comes before and what comes behind

A priori is Latin for "from what comes before" and *a posteriori* is Latin for "from what comes behind." So *a priori* knowledge is the kind that can be gained before, or without, sensory experience, and *a posteriori* knowledge is the kind that can be gained only after, or as a result of, sensory experience.

synthetic *a priori* knowledge?

And so to one of the biggest, most interesting questions in epistemology: can we have synthetic *a priori* knowledge?

Clearly, we can have analytic *a priori* knowledge—that is, we can come to know, through reason alone, things that are true by definition. And clearly, we can have synthetic *a posteriori* knowledge—that is, we can come to know, by investigating the world with our senses, matters of fact about the world. But can we have synthetic *a priori* knowledge? Can we come to know, through reason alone, matters of fact about the world outside our minds?

rationalism

Descartes, using his method of doubt, tried to free himself from all reliance upon the senses and to attain secure knowledge through the operation of the intellect alone. In epistemology, the view that reason is the principal source and test of knowledge is called "rationalism." The opposing view, that sensory experience is the principal source and test of knowledge, is known as "empiricism."

One of the key things on which rationalists and empiricists disagree is the issue of whether we can have synthetic *a priori* knowledge—whether we can have knowledge of the world outside our minds that's not based upon sensory experience.

Rationalists claim that we *can* achieve some knowledge of the world through reason alone, whereas empiricists contend that all knowledge of the world is ultimately derived from what we see, hear, touch, taste,

and smell. But what kinds of things do rationalists have in mind? What might we conceivably learn about the world outside our minds without the aid of our senses?

In Douglas Adams's *The Hitchhiker's Guide to the Galaxy*, the supercomputer Deep Thought is described as "so amazingly intelligent that even before its data banks had been connected up it had started from I think therefore I am and got as far as deducing the existence of rice pudding and income tax before anyone managed to turn it off." Is this the kind of synthetic *a priori* knowledge that rationalists have in mind? Well, not really. Not the bit about rice pudding and income tax anyway. Rationalists' claims to synthetic *a priori* knowledge tend to be much more general.

Parmenides

The first hardcore rationalist thinker in the Western world was the fifth-century-BCE Greek philosopher Parmenides, who based his entire philosophy on the fundamental precept that what is, is, and what is not, is not. From this self-evident truth, he deduced, via an ingenious if not entirely convincing chain of reasoning, that nothing ever moves and nothing ever changes (see box on page 76). He knew that the evidence of the senses flatly contradicts this, but he claimed that reason is superior to the senses, and therefore gets to be the arbiter of truth.

The world of moving, changing things revealed to us by the senses is mere illusion, he said. Only the intellect reveals the

rationalist philosophers

Apart from Parmenides and Descartes, philosophers who are traditionally thought of as rationalist include:

Plato (427–347 BCE)

According to Plato, we can never attain secure knowledge of the material world, that is, the changing world of sensory experience. The best we can do is to form opinions about it. There is, however, another realm, an unchanging world of nonmaterial entries, known as "the Forms." This world can be fully known and is accessible to reason rather than the senses.

Baruch Spinoza (1632–77)

Like all rationalists, Spinoza was impressed by the relentless logic of mathematical proofs. So much so that the arguments in his masterwork, the *Ethics*, are presented after the manner of geometrical theorems.

At the heart of Spinoza's metaphysics is the concept of substance, which he defines as that which does not depend on anything else for its existence. Given this definition, he argues that there can only be one such substance, "God or Nature." This means that everything is God, and God is everything.

God, here, is to be understood as abstract and impersonal, having no human attributes or qualities of any kind.

Gottfried Wilhelm Leibniz (1646–1716)

Through rational consideration of how things must be, Leibniz constructed a breathtaking, beautiful, and, it must be said, outrageously fanciful metaphysical system.

The world, he claimed, consists of an infinite number of non-material soul-like substances, known as "monads." These monads do not interact, but they appear to do so because God has perfectly synchronized their inner workings. Out of an infinite number of possible worlds, God created this one because it is the best of all possible worlds.

world as it really is. Parmenides, then, was a rationalist of an extreme kind. He held that reason is not merely the principal source of knowledge but the *only* source of knowledge. His assertions that nothing moves and nothing changes are claims to knowledge of the world acquired independently of (in fact, in direct contradiction to) sensory experience. In other words, they are claims to what we would now call synthetic *a priori* knowledge.

Parmenides's proofs

How did Parmenides deduce that nothing moves and nothing changes?

The precise form of his arguments is difficult to tease out from the few remaining fragments of his somewhat obscure writings, but the gist is as follows. If something were to move, then it would have to move into empty space. But empty space is nothing and doesn't exist—what is not, is not—so nothing moves. Whenever you think, you think *of* something, and anything you can think of must exist—what is not, is not, so it can't be the object of thought. But anything you think of, you can think of in precisely the same way at any time. Therefore it must exist in precisely the same way at all times. So nothing changes.

Descartes revisited

The first great rationalist of the modern period was Descartes. Parmenides built his rationalist philosophy upon the fundamental precept that what is, is, and what is not, is not. In a similar fashion, in the 17th century, Descartes built his own rationalist philosophy upon the fundamental precept of the cogito ("I think, therefore I am."). Here's how he did it…

clear and distinct ideas

Having identified in the cogito his first item of indubitable knowledge, Descartes asked himself what it was that made it indubitable. The answer, it seemed to him, was simply that it *had* to be true.

As soon he pondered the cogito, he understood that it couldn't be false. It was an idea that was, in his own phraseology, so "clear and distinct" that it couldn't be denied. It didn't need any supporting evidence or argument. He could simply hold it in his mind and see that there was no alternative to its being true. In the *Meditations* Descartes writes:

In this first item of knowledge there is simply a clear and distinct perception of what I am asserting; this would not be enough to make

me certain of the truth of the matter if it could ever turn out that something which I perceived with such clarity and distinctness was false. **So I now seem to be able to lay it down as a general rule that whatever I perceive very clearly and distinctly is true.**

This was a huge insight, because it opened up the possibility that there might be other ideas that were equally clear and distinct. And if there were, Descartes reasoned, then those ideas couldn't be doubted either. Very conveniently, it turned out that there was such another idea: the idea of God.

a perfect being

Descartes discovered, by introspection, that in his mind he had the idea of a perfect being: a being unlimited, eternal, boundless, lacking nothing, the creator and maintainer of all things. In short, God. When he examined this idea, he saw clearly and distinctly that such a being must exist not only in his mind but also in reality. From the very idea of God, it followed with absolute certainty that God exists.

In the *Meditations*, he provides two justifications for this claim. The first of these is Descartes's spin on an argument originally devised in the 12th century by St. Anselm. This is the so-called ontological argument, which we will examine in due course (see pages 88–91).

The second, which was Descartes's own invention, is often referred to as the trademark argument. Put briefly and rather crudely, it runs as follows. I have in my mind the idea of a perfect being, but where did this idea come from? It couldn't have come from me, since I am an imperfect being. No, it could only have come from a being that was itself perfect. So the idea of God, which I find in my mind, must have been put there by God himself as a kind of "trademark" or stamp of manufacture.

This argument relies upon a philosophical principle, which was widely accepted at the time, that there must be at least as much reality in a cause as there is in its effect. This means, or so Descartes claimed, that if an idea is perfect, then its cause must be perfect, too.

Few philosophers find Descartes's ontological and trademark arguments convincing. But Descartes himself was so taken with them that he felt he could no more doubt God's existence than he could doubt his own. Furthermore, he found that he could no more doubt God's attributes—such as His unlimited power, wisdom, and benevolence—than he could doubt God's existence. This is because God is, by definition, a *perfect* being, and a being that was limited in power, wisdom, benevolence, or any other good thing would be an *imperfect* being.

neither dream nor delusion

Descartes, then, claimed indubitable knowledge of the existence of a supremely powerful, wise, and benevolent being: God.

Descartes's legacy

Descartes isn't called "the father of modern philosophy" for nothing. The ideas and arguments he put forward in the *Meditations* marked a watershed in the history of thought. After Descartes, philosophy cast off the shackles of Aristotelianism and Scholasticism and set off in an entirely new direction. The issues he raised became philosophy's main preoccupations from the second half of the 17th century onward. In particular:

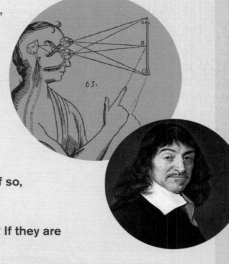

- **The problem of the external world.**
  Can we have knowledge of the external world? If so, how do we acquire it?
- **The mind–body problem.**
  Is the mind part of the body, or are they distinct? If they are distinct, how do they interact? (See chapter 7.)

This doesn't mean that Descartes's contemporaries and successors agreed with everything he said. Far from it. Almost all of his arguments have been roundly criticized and, for the most part, rejected.

There's a general consensus of opinion that Descartes did a sterling job with the destructive phase of his *Meditations*, that he succeeded, through his method of doubt, in identifying lots of interesting and important problems. But there's also a consensus of opinion that he failed in the constructive phase.

Up to and including the cogito, his arguments are, on the whole, rather compelling, but from his proofs of the existence of God onward they lose their force.

Descartes's ambition had been to clear away the errors of the past and rebuild the edifice of human knowledge upon secure foundations. He felt that he had achieved this, but he is generally regarded as having failed to overcome his own skeptical arguments.

As Bertrand Russell states in *A History of Western Philosophy*: "Modern philosophy has very largely accepted the formulation of its problems from Descartes, while not accepting his solutions."

It was inconceivable, Descartes reasoned, that such a being would ever deceive his creatures or would ever allow them to be deceived.

This being the case, Descartes decided that he could be confident that the material world is neither a dream nor a delusion, and that he could trust his own God-given powers of reason provided he was careful to exercise them with due diligence.

Of course, he must take care never to jump to conclusions; never to make hasty judgments about the world based merely on appearances. He should always think carefully and scientifically about how to interpret his sensory experiences. But, nonetheless, with sufficient care, he could attain reliable knowledge of the world.

the supremacy of reason

So after freeing himself from all reliance upon the senses, Descartes demonstrated to his own satisfaction that he himself existed, that God existed, that the senses reliably informed him of the existence of an external world, and that, provided he proceeded cautiously and carefully, he could attain, through the joint operation of reason and the senses, reliable knowledge of that world.

This entire system of knowledge was built upon a foundation of self-evident truths, including the cogito and the existence of a perfect being, which were revealed by reason rather than the senses. The senses had a role to play in the acquisition of knowledge, but it was a

a thinking thing

In the *Meditations*, as soon as he had established *that* he is, Descartes set to musing upon *what* he is. He had derived "I am" from "I think." This implied that he was, first and foremost, a thinking thing:

At last I have discovered it—thought; this alone is inseparable from me. I am, I exist—that is certain. But for how long? For as long as I am thinking. For it could be that were I totally to cease from thinking, I should totally cease to exist... I am, then, in the strict sense only a thing that thinks; that is, I am a mind, or intelligence...

He could doubt that he had a body, but he couldn't doubt that he had a mind. Therefore his mind and body—assuming, for the moment, that he *had* a body—must be two distinct things.

secondary one. The primary role belonged to reason, which was the ultimate source and test of knowledge.

Descartes's assertion that God necessarily exists is a claim to knowledge of the world outside the mind acquired independently of the senses. That is, it is a claim to synthetic *a priori* knowledge.

empiricism

As we learned in the previous section, rationalists view reason as the principle source and test of knowledge. In seeking to understand the nature of reality, they begin by trying to identify *a priori* certainties. That is, by thinking hard about how things must be. Empiricists, on the other hand, regard sensory experience as the principle source and test of knowledge. They seek to understand the world by first looking about them and then reflecting upon what they see.

John Locke (1632–1704) is widely regarded as the greatest-ever English philosopher. His *Essay Concerning Human Understanding* is one of philosophy's most influential works, and his *Two Treatises of Government* has been enormously influential in the wider world of politics. He was friends with the scientists Isaac Newton and Robert Boyle, and was a thoroughgoing empiricist.

He held that everything we can know must ultimately be derived from experience.

Locke's empiricism

Locke believed that one of the biggest sources of error in the philosophy of his time was the widely held doctrine of innate ideas, that is, the belief that certain ideas are implanted in the mind prior to birth. Contrary to this, he maintained that when a child is born it knows nothing. It has no thoughts and no ideas. Its mind is as empty as a blank sheet of paper.

In the *Essay*, he writes:

> **Let us suppose the mind to be, as we say, white paper, void of all characters, without any ideas; how comes it to be furnished? Whence comes it by that vast store which the busy and boundless fancy of man has painted on it with an almost endless variety? Whence has it all the materials of reason and knowledge? To this I answer, in one word, from** *experience*.

As the child develops, the blank sheet of its mind gets written upon by the pen of experience. Experience comes in two ways. First, through what Locke calls sensation—through the senses of sight, hearing, touch, taste, and smell—and, second, through what he calls reflexion—that is, through the mind's consciousness of its own operations.

So, first of all, the child acquires the idea of red through seeing red things, the idea of loud through hearing loud things, the idea of hot by touching hot things, the idea of sweet though tasting sweet things, the idea of pain though the sensory experience of pain, and so on. Then, as the child develops, it begins to acquire another set of ideas by introspection. So, from the experience of thinking it learns what thinking is, from the experience of desiring it learns what desire is, from the experience of doubting it learns what doubting is, and so on.

Everything we can know or think ultimately derives from ideas we acquire through these two kinds of experience. But the mind is no passive receptacle for these ideas. It works upon them, comparing, analyzing, ordering, organizing, abstracting, and compounding them. One of the most remarkable and useful features of the mind is its ability to create complex ideas from simple components—that is, to combine the simple ideas we acquire from sensation and reflection in new and creative ways. For example, although I have never seen a golden castle, I can easily form the idea of one by combining the ideas I have of gold and of castles.

The mind can do all kinds of creative and interesting things with the ideas it acquires through experience. But prior to experience it has no ideas to work with.

the idea of God

As we saw in the previous section, one of the key features of Descartes's rationalist philosophy was his claim that the idea of God is innate, that the idea of an unlimited being couldn't have originated in his own finite mind but must have been planted there by God Himself.

Locke disagreed. He argued that the complex idea of God can easily be formed by combining together simpler ideas derived from experience. All we have to do is take ideas such as power, knowledge, and benevolence, which we acquire by observing other people and ourselves, and then combine them with the idea of an increase without limit. In a similar fashion, Locke argued that all of the other ideas traditionally regarded as innate—self-evident logical precepts, ideas of right and wrong and suchlike—were, in fact, derived from experience.

three kinds of knowledge

As stated previously, by Locke's account, the mind is no passive receptacle of ideas. It has the ability to analyze them, compare them, order them, and so forth. In other words, it can think about them. This ability to discern the relationship between ideas is what Locke means by knowledge.

In the *Essay*, Locke identifies three kinds of knowledge: intuitive, demonstrative, and sensitive. Intuitive knowledge is acquired when the mind "perceives the agreement or disagreement of two ideas immediately by themselves." It is through intuition, Locke says, that the mind perceives that white is not black, that a circle is not a triangle, that three are more than two.

This is the most certain kind of knowledge that we fallible humans can have.

Demonstrative knowledge derives from the mind's ability to deduce certain kinds of truths, such as those of geometry and arithmetic, by a sequence of intuitions. It is the kind of knowledge we acquire when we start from intuitively certain premises and reason our way to more complex truths. Pythagoras' Theorem and the Fundamental Theorem of Arithmetic (that any integer above 1 is either prime itself or is the product of prime numbers) are examples of this kind of knowledge. Demonstrative knowledge has a high degree of certainty, but it is not as certain as intuitive knowledge, since it requires effort and attention to follow the steps required to get from premises to conclusions.

Lastly, sensitive knowledge is knowledge of the world that we acquire through the senses—or, as Locke puts it, "knowledge of particular external objects, by that perception and consciousness we have of the actual entrance of ideas from them." This is the least certain form of knowledge. In fact, it doesn't really count as knowledge at all, not in the strictest sense of the world. This is because the only thing that assures us of the existence of external objects is their acting upon our senses to produce ideas. But there is an element of doubt about this because sometimes we have sensory ideas—while dreaming, for example—for which there is no corresponding external object.

Nonetheless, sensitive knowledge, although not entirely certain, is secure enough for most practical purposes and therefore "passes under the name of knowledge" after all.

the primacy of sense-experience

Locke's view that intuitive and demonstrative knowledge are more certain than sensitive knowledge seems, at first glance, more rationalist than empiricist. But his empiricist credentials remain intact since he holds that no intuitive or demonstrative knowledge is possible until the mind has some materials to work with. And these materials derive from experience. Thus, the mind can't intuit that blue is not green until it has acquired the ideas of blue and green, and it can't demonstrate that one plus two is three until it has acquired, through experience, the concepts one, two, and three. The human mind has a capacity for comparing, analyzing, and compounding ideas, but, in the absence of experience, it has no ideas to work with.

Like all good empiricists, Locke holds that no knowledge of the world is possible without sensory experience. In other words, there is no synthetic *a priori* knowledge. And, in fact, he goes further than that. He claims that no knowledge of any kind is possible until the mind is furnished with ideas acquired through experience.

empiricist philosophers

Apart from Locke, philosophers traditionally thought of as empiricist include:

Francis Bacon (1561–1626)

Francis Bacon was not only a philosopher but also a lawyer, a scientist, and a statesman. From 1618–21 he served as Lord Chancellor of England.

As a philosopher and scientist, he was preoccupied with the question of how mankind can acquire secure and useful knowledge. His own answer to this question was, through the method of induction (see page 37)— that is, through testing and refining hypotheses by observing, measuring, and experimenting.

Bacon has been called the founder of empiricism and is regarded as one of the founders of scientific method.

George Berkeley (1685–1753)

Berkeley was an Irish philosopher and bishop. He claimed that nothing in our experience justifies us in believing in the existence of an external world. In fact, he went further than that, and argued that the entire notion of an external world is absurd.

According to Berkeley, the only things that exist are minds and their ideas. So-called material objects are really just collections of ideas— ideas in our minds and, more importantly, ideas in the mind of God.

David Hume (1711–76)

The Scottish philosopher David Hume argued that human knowledge is limited to sense-experience. He claimed that not even our most basic beliefs about the world can be rationally justified, not even our beliefs in the existence of the external world, the reality of cause and effect, or the existence of the self.

We do and must believe these things, but our beliefs are based not upon reason but on upon accumulated experience, upon habit and instinct.

what is metaphysics?

defining metaphysics

Aristotle defined metaphysics as "[The] science which studies being *qua* being, and the attributes belonging to it in its own right." This is a good definition but perhaps a bit abstruse for our purposes. A more helpful way of putting it might be to say that metaphysics is the study of *what* there is and the *ultimate nature* of what there is.

At first glance, this seems scarcely more helpful. But we can shed some light on it by actually doing some metaphysics and asking ourselves what kinds of stuff the world is made from and what that stuff is like.

what there is

We can begin to answer these questions by listing everyday objects such as rocks, rivers, mountains, stars, planets, people, fish, and so on.

Then, thinking back to high-school science, we might decide to include the building blocks of matter such as atoms, protons, neutrons, and electrons.

Some people might want to stop there, but others would argue that the list is incomplete, since it doesn't include nonphysical objects such as minds, spirits, souls, angels, and God, for example.

And what about mathematical objects such as numbers and shapes? Do circles, squares, the number 13, the square root of two, pi, and suchlike exist? Are they part of the furniture of the universe? Or are they merely mental constructs?

Following this line of thought, we might pause to consider whether to include fictional characters like Harry Potter or Ebenezer Scrooge in our list. After all, if they don't exist, how is it that we can talk about them?

And what about properties such as red, smooth, and cold? Do redness, smoothness, and coldness exist? If so, in what sense? Do they exist in the same way that chairs, clouds, and helium atoms do? Or do they have a different kind of existence?

the ultimate nature of what there is

So far we have been considering the fundamental metaphysical question of what kinds of stuff the world contains. We could go on to think about the nature of all that stuff. For example, we might take the view that the world contains both minds and bodies and that these are distinct categories of being. If so, we could ask ourselves what are the defining characteristics of each and what relationship they have with one another. (More on these questions in chapter 7.)

The investigation of what types of things there are, and the relationships they have to one another, is known as "ontology." It is the central branch of metaphysics.

questions of metaphysics

In this short chapter we will only get to dip our toes into the ocean that is metaphysics, by exploring a few ideas in ontology. But, in fact, metaphysicians puzzle over a huge variety of questions. Here are a few of them:

- What is existence?
- Does the world exist outside of the mind?
- What are numbers?
- Does God exist?
- Is everything that happens predetermined?
- How is change possible?
- What makes me the same person today that I was yesterday?
- Do we have free will?
- Do humans have souls?

- What is space?
- What is time?
- Why is there something rather than nothing?
- What are laws of nature?
- What is consciousness?

Aristotle's metaphysics

The word "metaphysics" has its origin in the works of Aristotle (384–22 BCE). In ancient times, when the great philosopher's works were collected and edited (probably by Andronicus of Rhodes in the first century BCE) the treatises following those on physics were called the metaphysics—the Greek word *meta* meaning "after." So, in this context, metaphysics simply means "the works following on from those on physics."

Aristotle's metaphysics included three areas of study:

- **Ontology (the study of being and existence)**
- **Natural theology (the study of God, "the highest kind of being")**
- **Universal science (the study of first principles that are true of every existing thing)**

Aristotle himself never used the term "metaphysics." He tended to refer to this class of questions as "first philosophy."

the ontological argument

Metaphysics can be thought of as the attempt to discover what exists and to understand the nature of what exists.

One of the metaphysical problems that has most exercised philosophers during the past two and a half thousand years concerns the existence and nature of God. "Does God exist?" and "What kind of being is God?" are questions that have preoccupied many of history's great thinkers.

The case for and against God will be explored in some detail in chapter 6. For the present, however, we will examine just one famous and influential argument regarding the existence and nature of God, the so-called "ontological argument," devised by St. Anselm in the 11th century.

The greatest conceivable being

In his philosophical and theological work the *Proslogion*, Anselm presented what he considered to be an irrefutable argument for the existence of God.

Our concept of God, he said, is that of "a being than which nothing greater can be conceived." Does such a being exist? Some people think not. As the Bible puts it: "The fool has said in his heart, there is no God."

But, although the fool denies the existence of God, he understands the concept of God:

> But, at any rate, this very fool, when he hears of this being of which I speak—a being than which nothing greater can be conceived—understands what he hears, and what he understands is in his understanding; although he does not understand it to exist.

So the fool admits that the greatest conceivable being exists in his mind, if nowhere else.

But a thing that exists in reality is greater than a thing that exists only in the mind. Thus, if the greatest conceivable being were to exist only in the mind, then it would be possible to conceive a greater one. Namely that same being existing in reality.

St. Anselm of Canterbury

Anselm (1033–1109) was a theologian and philosopher. He was born in Italy, served as a monk and then as prior at a monastery in Bec in Normandy, and was eventually appointed Archbishop of Canterbury (the senior bishop in England). After his death he was canonized, although precisely when is unknown.

In addition to a deep Christian faith, Anselm had a passion for philosophical argument. This combination led to his adoption of a distinctive approach to theology, that of faith seeking understanding. "I do not seek to understand so that I may believe," he wrote, "but I believe so that I may understand."

In philosophy, Anselm's chief aim was to clarify and reinforce the teachings of the Scriptures by means of reasoned argument. With this purpose in mind he wrote two treatises, the *Monologion* and the *Proslogion*, in which he applied his distinctive method to theological subjects such as the incarnation, redemption, free will, and the existence and nature of God.

This meant that he didn't approach the question of God's nature and existence in a spirit of detached inquiry. Quite the reverse. He already believed, upon the authority of the Scriptures and Church doctrine, that God exists and that He is omnipotent, omniscient, and omnibenevolent. What he sought was intellectual justification for those beliefs.

Gaunilo's island

The first major criticism of Anselm's argument came from a monk called Gaunilo. He objected that you could adopt precisely the same kind of reasoning to demonstrate the existence of all kinds of crazy things—the greatest conceivable island, for example.

The idea of the greatest conceivable island is perfectly comprehensible, says Gaunilo. Therefore it exists in your understanding. And since it is more excellent to exist in reality than it is to exist in the understanding alone, the island must really exist. "For if it does not exist, any land which really exists will be more excellent than it; and so the island already understood by you to be more excellent will not be more excellent."

Gaunilo's point was that it would be absurd to argue this way. You can't simply magic an island into existence by thinking about it. And if the island argument is absurd, then Anselm's argument about God must be absurd, too.

Anselm responded that the argument applies only to God. This is because the concept of God, the greatest conceivable being, is a perfectly clear and intelligible one, whereas the concept of the greatest conceivable island isn't.

If we were asked to list the properties of the greatest conceivable island, we wouldn't even know what to include. So, unlike the concept of God, we have no clear understanding of it. It doesn't exist inside or outside of the understanding.

But that would mean conceiving of a being greater than the greatest conceivable being, which is impossible. It's a logical contradiction. And the only way to avoid it is to accept that God exists not only in the mind but also in reality.

Therefore, if that, than which nothing greater can be conceived, exists in the understanding alone, the very being, than which nothing greater can be conceived, is one, than which a greater can be conceived. But obviously this is impossible. Hence, there is no doubt that there exists a being, than which nothing greater can be conceived, and it exists both in the understanding and in reality.

This is quite a long and involved argument. The gist of it is that since it's better to exist in reality than it is to exist only in the mind, the greatest conceivable being must exist in reality.

A simpler way of putting it would to say that God is, by definition, a perfect being, and a being isn't perfect if it doesn't exist, therefore, God, by definition, exists.

Furthermore, the "being than which nothing greater can be conceived" must have all of the attributes that it's good to have and must have them all in the highest degree. Otherwise it would be possible to conceive of a greater being. This means that God must be supremely good, powerful, wise, just, merciful, and so on.

Kant's objection

The most famous, and probably the most damning, objection to the ontological argument came centuries later, from the German philosopher Immanuel Kant (1724–1804). He said that Anselm's mistake was in treating existence as a property when, in fact, it isn't.

According to Kant, when we ascribe properties to a thing, we *presuppose* its existence. For example, if you were to ask me to give a description of my wife, you'd expect me to say things like, "She's five feet two. She has brown hair and brown eyes. She weighs 114 pounds. She likes sushi," and so on. You wouldn't expect me to add, "She exists." That would be presupposed.

When we say that something exists, we don't add anything to the concept of that thing. We merely claim that there is something in the world corresponding to that concept.

So, although the concept of God, as the greatest conceivable being, necessarily includes properties such as omnipotence, omniscience, and the like, it doesn't include existence. Because existence isn't a property. You don't add anything to the concept of God by saying that God exists. You merely claim that the concept of God is instantiated.

Or, as Kant put it: "When I think of a being as the supreme reality, without any defect, the question still remains whether it exists or not."

Plato & the forms

One of the best-known and most influential metaphysical theories in the history of Western philosophy was advanced by Plato (427–347 BCE).

Plato said that the everyday world, the one we apprehend through the senses, isn't real. It's just shadows and illusion. He argued for the existence of a timeless, unchanging world of what he called forms—a realm of truth, beauty, and ultimate reality.

Plato

If you were to ask the man or woman in the street to name a philosopher, they'd almost certainly say Plato. He is the most famous and probably the most influential philosopher of all time. But, despite his fame, relatively little is known for certain about his life.

Plato was a pupil and admirer of Socrates, and was present at the trial of Socrates in 399 BCE (see page 22). He came from an aristocratic and well-connected Athenian family, and as a young man he envisioned a political career for himself. However, following Socrates's death, he became disillusioned with politics and turned his talents to philosophy instead.

After Socrates's trial, Plato traveled around the Mediterranean for a number of years. When he returned to Athens, around 385 BCE, he founded a school, known as the Academy, where the sons of aristocratic families could study mathematics, astronomy, and philosophy. The Academy is generally considered to be the world's first university, hence the English word "academic." Its most celebrated pupil was Aristotle, the only philosopher whose influence on Western thought rivals Plato's own.

Plato, unlike Socrates, who wrote nothing of his philosophy down, left behind a large body of work, presented mostly in dialogue form. He was a gifted poet and dramatist, and his writings are regarded as works of literary as well as philosophical brilliance.

Plato's dialogues often feature Socrates as the main protagonist. In the early ones, the character Socrates is thought to portray the historical Socrates's philosophical ideas fairly accurately, but in the middle and later dialogues, he becomes more and more a mouthpiece for Plato's own ideas.

the theory of forms

Prior to Plato, a number of Greek philosophers had noted that the world, as it appears to the senses, is constantly changing. This caused some of them to question its reality. Parmenides, for example, went so far as to claim that the world of the senses is mere illusion and that only the intellect reveals the world as it really is (see pages 74–76).

Plato developed this idea in his famous Theory of Forms, which holds that ultimate reality is timeless and changeless and can be perceived only by the intellect.

Everything we perceive with our senses is changing and imperfect, said Plato. For example, the sensory world contains many instances of circles: the disc of the sun, the circumference of a dinner plate, the eye of a daisy, drawings produced with compasses. However, none of these things is perfectly circular, and none of these things endures forever.

But although we can never see or touch a perfect circle, we *can* form the idea of one. Intellectually, we can conceive of a round, two-dimensional figure, the boundary of which consists of points equidistant from a fixed point.

how Aristocles became Plato

Plato's talents were more than just intellectual. He had a powerful physique and was so skilled a wrestler that he is said to have competed at the prestigious Isthmian Games.

The name Plato—from the Greek *platon*, meaning "broad"—was actually given to him by his wrestling coach on account of his broad shoulders. His birth name was in fact Aristocles.

This abstract entity, which Plato calls the Idea or Form of the Circle, is perfect and eternal and therefore fully real. It doesn't exist in the physical world. It doesn't exist in space and time. But, according to Plato, it does exist in another realm, in the timeless, unchanging realm of the forms.

Here's another example. The sensory world contains many beautiful objects—flowers, sunsets, women, etc.—but none of these things is unchangingly and perfectly beautiful. Even the loveliest, freshest rose has some imperfections, however slight, and its beauty quickly fades.

tableness and cupness

In the third century CE, Diogenes Laërtius, in his *Lives and Opinions of Eminent Philosophers* (an entertaining if unreliable biography of the Greek philosophers), gave an amusing account of a supposed conversation between Plato and the philosopher Diogenes on the subject of the forms. He wrote:

"Plato was discoursing about his 'Ideas,' and using the nouns 'tableness' and 'cupness' 'Plato!' interrupted Diogenes, 'I see a table and a cup, but I see no tableness or cupness.' Plato replied, 'That is natural enough, for you have eyes, by which a cup and a table are contemplated; but you have not intellect, by which tableness and cupness are seen.'"

But, intellectually, we can conceive of the thing that all beautiful objects share, namely the quality of beauty, which Plato called "Beauty itself." This, Plato insisted, is perfectly and unchangingly beautiful—and, what's more, it's real. It exists. Just as there is a Form of the Circle, so there is a Form of Beauty.

the world of forms

There is, Plato claimed, a whole world of forms.

Just as there is a Form of the Circle, there's also a Form of the Square, a Form of the Triangle, a Form of the Number Seven, a Form of Odd Numbers, and so on. And just as there is a Form of Beauty, there's also a Form of Justice, a Form of Truth, a Form of Goodness. There are even forms of physical objects, such as tables, cups, cats, dogs, and trees. This is because, in addition to all of the individual tables, cups, cats, dogs, and trees in the world, which are imperfect and changeable, and which go in and out of existence, there are also the abstract concepts of tableness, cupness, catness, dogness, and treeness which are eternal and unchanging.

the allegory of the cave

The Theory of Forms takes some getting your head around. Plato was aware of this, and so, in his most celebrated work, *The Republic*, he used an allegory to help explain it.

He wrote:

arguments for the forms

What were Plato's reasons for believing in the existence of the forms?

Surprisingly, he didn't provide any clear supporting arguments. He just had a number of intuitive reasons for thinking that they must exist. For example, in addition to being able to talk about individual beautiful objects, we can also talk about the common feature that these objects share, namely beauty. But if we can think and talk about beauty, then it must exist, otherwise how could we refer to it or contemplate it?

Nothing in the sensory world is unqualifiedly beautiful. So, one woman might be beautiful compared with other women but not when compared with a goddess. Despite this, we understand what absolute beauty is. We have a standard by which to judge the beauty of individual objects. This must be because we have some acquaintance with "Beauty itself."

the philosopher king

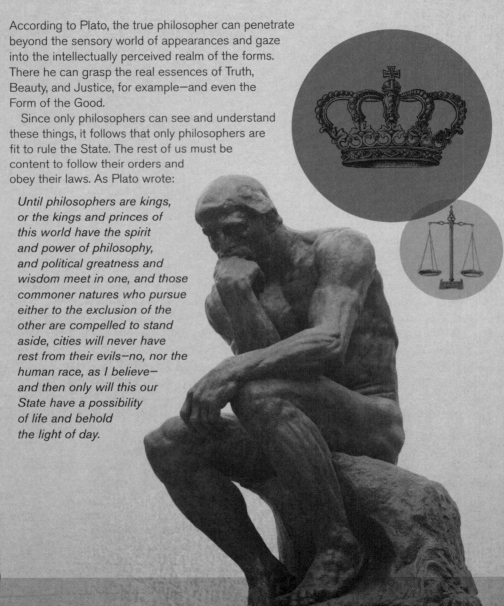

According to Plato, the true philosopher can penetrate beyond the sensory world of appearances and gaze into the intellectually perceived realm of the forms. There he can grasp the real essences of Truth, Beauty, and Justice, for example—and even the Form of the Good.

Since only philosophers can see and understand these things, it follows that only philosophers are fit to rule the State. The rest of us must be content to follow their orders and obey their laws. As Plato wrote:

Until philosophers are kings, or the kings and princes of this world have the spirit and power of philosophy, and political greatness and wisdom meet in one, and those commoner natures who pursue either to the exclusion of the other are compelled to stand aside, cities will never have rest from their evils—no, nor the human race, as I believe—and then only will this our State have a possibility of life and behold the light of day.

Behold! human beings living in an underground cave... Here they have been from their childhood, and have their legs and necks chained so that they cannot move, and can only see before them, being prevented by the chains from turning round their heads.

Behind the prisoners is a fire, and in front of them—the only thing that they can see—is the cave wall.

Their captors use the firelight to project shadows of puppets and various objects on to the wall, and the prisoners, seeing nothing but the shadows, take them for reality. They think that the shadow world is the real world.

Then, one day, one of the prisoners is unshackled. He turns around. At first he is dazzled by the firelight. But, when his eyes adjust, he discovers that the world he had taken for reality was just an illusion. He sees the true cause of the shadows.

Later, he is taken outside into the sunlit world. Once again, he is dazzled at first, but when his eyes adjust, he sees that he is now in a world more real and more beautiful than the world of shadows. After a long time above ground, his eyes become so accustomed to the light that he is able to gaze upon the sun itself.

knowledge and the forms

In the allegory of the cave, the shackled prisoners represent the human race, the shadows in the cave represent the sensory world, the world of appearances, and the unshackled prisoner represents the philosopher.

Most people spend their entire lives taking the world of appearances for reality. They see beautiful objects, but they never see Beauty itself. They never even imagine that such a thing exists. They see individual examples of justice, truth, and goodness, but they never see beyond those things to Justice, Truth, and Goodness themselves. But the philosopher, like the prisoner freed from his chains, learns to see beyond appearances.

The philosopher's enlightenment comes in two stages.

First, he learns to contemplate individual forms, such as the Form of the Circle and the Form of Beauty. This is represented in the allegory by the unshackled prisoner seeing the objects that cast the shadows on the cave wall.

Second, he learns to contemplate the ultimate form, the Form of the Good. This is the source of everything that is right and beautiful in the sensory world and the source of reason and truth in the intellectual world. It is represented in the allegory by the sun.

realism & idealism

One of the most important debates in metaphysics is that between realists and idealists. *Realism* is the view that objects in the world exist independently of our thoughts and perceptions of them. *Idealism* is the opposing view, that everything that exists is mental, that the things we think of as material objects are really ideas in minds.

Realists claim that there is a world of material objects out there and that those objects are there whether we perceive them or not. If every sentient being were suddenly to die, they would remain there regardless. This view accords very well with common sense. It's taken as a given by most people who haven't studied or thought a great deal about philosophy.

Most people take realism a step farther and take the view that objects really are the way they appear to be. So bananas not only appear to be yellow, they *are* yellow. Similarly, oranges really are round, lemons really are bitter, coconuts really are hard, and so on. This version of realism is known as "common-sense realism."

However plausible it may seem at first, common-sense realism doesn't hold up too well to philosophical scrutiny. So, although many philosophers are realists, few philosophers are common-sense realists.

Locke on primary and secondary qualities

A major problem with the view that the objects in the world are just the way they appear to be was identified by the empiricist philosopher John Locke (see page 80).

Locke was a realist. He didn't doubt that there is an external world which is known to us through sense perception. But he rejected the notion that objects in the external world are just as they appear to be. Here's why.

Material objects, he said, have the power to act upon our senses and produce ideas in our minds. A snowball, for example, has the power to produce in us ideas of cold, round, white, firm, and so on. He called these powers qualities.

He then made a distinction between two different types of qualities, which he labeled primary qualities and secondary qualities.

Primary qualities include shape, size, number, and motion. Locke said that these qualities really exist in objects. So, a snowball is made up of a certain number of constituent parts, each of which has a certain size, shape, and motion. And the snowball itself, being an aggregate of those parts, also has genuine properties of size, shape, and motion. Furthermore, Locke said that the ideas we have in our minds of primary qualities resemble those qualities in objects themselves. When we see a snowball as round, for example, that's because it really *is* round.

Secondary qualities include colors, sounds, tastes, and smells. Unlike primary qualities, these don't exist in objects themselves. Consider the snowball again. It looks white, but the whiteness isn't really a feature of the snowball. It's a feature of our visual experience. Although in a loose sense we can say that a snowball is white, what this really means is that a snowball has the power to produce in us, when viewed under suitable conditions, a sensation of whiteness. There's no whiteness in the snowball itself.

The same kind of reasoning applies to the other secondary qualities. Locke said that the secondary qualities of objects are to be understood in terms of their primary qualities. Our ideas of secondary qualities derive from the interaction of our sensory apparatus with objects by virtue of their primary qualities. Thus, we see a snowball as white because of the way its constituent parts—by reason of their particular size, shape, and motion—interact, via the medium of light, with our eyes. (We would now put this in terms of its atomic and molecular structure, but the basic idea still stands.) The upshot of all of this is that secondary qualities are mind-dependent. If all sentient beings were to die, secondary qualities would cease to exist. In Locke's words:

The ideas of the primary [qualities] alone really exist. The particular bulk, number, figure, and motion of the parts of fire or snow are really in them, whether anyone's senses perceive them or no: and therefore they may be called real qualities, because they really exist in those bodies. But light, heat, whiteness, or coldness, are no more really in them

than sickness or pain is in manna [a laxative]. Take away the sensation of them; let not the eyes see light or colours, nor the ears hear sounds; let the palate not taste, nor the nose smell, and all colours, tastes, odours, and sounds, as they are such particular ideas, vanish and cease, and are reduced to their causes, i.e. bulk, figure, and motion of parts.

representative realism

So, according to Locke, there is an external world, but we only ever experience it indirectly. There's a causal process by which the primary qualities of objects act upon our senses to produce ideas in our minds, and these ideas represent the world to us.

When we examine a banana, for example, what we are aware of isn't the banana itself but a kind of inner representation or model of it. This model is pretty accurate as far as primary qualities are concerned, since our ideas of primary qualities resemble actual features of objects. But the inner model isn't accurate with regard to the secondary qualities. It represents the banana as having a certain color, taste, and smell, but none of those things is really in the banana.

So, although Locke was a realist, he wasn't a common-sense realist. He believed that there is a real world that exists independently of our minds, but he didn't accept that external objects are just as they appear to us to be.

The theory that physical objects are perceived indirectly via mental images or representations is known to philosophers today as representative realism. Locke was one of the first to adopt such a theory.

Berkeley on primary and secondary qualities

The 18th-century philosopher George Berkeley didn't accept the primary/secondary quality distinction. He argued that Locke's so-called primary qualities are every bit as mind-dependent as his so-called secondary qualities.

Take shape, for example. What evidence do we have for claiming that an object such as a snowball is round? Only that it *looks* round and *feels* round. We could take measurements, of course, but we would still have to rely on our senses of sight and touch in order to make and interpret those measurements. Take away those sensations, Berkeley argued, and no idea of roundness remains. The only way we can think about shape is in terms of sensory ideas.

Locke claimed that our ideas of shape accurately represent features of external objects, but Berkeley asked how he could possibly know this. All of our ideas regarding the shapes of objects are based on how they look and feel. But we have no way of checking that the way they look and feel is the way they really are.

Berkeley's idealism

Locke's theory of perception was fatally flawed, Berkeley insisted. It claimed that our ideas represent the world to us

Bishop Berkeley

George Berkeley (1685–1753) was born in Ireland, although he was of English descent. At age 15, he went to Trinity College in Dublin, Ireland, where he received a thorough grounding in the most up-to-date ideas in science and philosophy.

After graduating, he published, during a four-year burst of productivity, three short but important philosophical works: *An Essay Towards a New Theory of Vision*; *A Treatise Concerning the Principles of Human Knowledge;* and *Three Dialogues between Hylas and Philonous.*

The *Treatise* and the *Three Dialogues* contain Berkeley's arguments for immaterialism and idealism and are the works for which he is best remembered. The *Dialogues* is the shorter of the two, is generally considered easier to follow, and, because it is presented in dialogue form and beautifully written, is actually quite a fun read.

In 1713, Berkeley moved to England, where he befriended some of the country's literary elite, including the writers Alexander Pope and Jonathan Swift. Later, he traveled in Europe and America, and tried unsuccessfully to establish a missionary college in Bermuda. In 1734, he was appointed Bishop of Cloyne, in Ireland.

In his later years, he devoted much of his energy to promoting the health-giving properties of tar-water, an evil-smelling concoction made from pine-water and tar. He claimed that a pint of tar-water a day would cure almost every disease.

arguments against materialism

Berkeley's immaterialism—his denial of the existence of matter—is very counterintuitive. But he advanced a number of arguments in support of his strange-sounding thesis.

Matter is an empty concept.

All we know about the objects in the world is how they look, sound, feel, taste, and smell. But these are all "ideas of sense." Take these ideas away and nothing remains. So all talk of "matter" and "material objects" is, in fact, empty talk. It has no meaning.

Matter is unnecessary.

The materialists of Berkeley's time claimed that God creates material objects, which act upon our senses to produce ideas in our minds. But God can just as easily place those ideas directly into our minds. So matter is redundant.

Matter is inconceivable.

The materialist claims that matter is something that can exist unperceived. But the very idea of something existing unperceived is absurd. However hard we try to conceive of something, say a tree, existing unperceived, we will fail. For in the very act of trying, we think of, or perceive, that very thing! Matter is therefore a contradictory, and hence impossible, notion.

accurately in some important respects—that is, in respect of primary qualities—but there is no evidence to back up this claim. We have no way of knowing whether *any* of our ideas accurately represent external objects. In fact, we have no reason to suppose that our ideas are caused by external objects at all.

"When we do our utmost to conceive the existence of external bodies, we are all the while only contemplating our own ideas," said Berkeley. This insight led him to make the startling claim that the entire notion of a material world existing independently of the mind is best abandoned. Accordingly, Berkeley developed a view of reality which consists only of minds and ideas. This is sometimes labeled "immaterialism," because it denies the existence of matter; it is also called idealism because it holds that everything that exists is mental.

minds and ideas

According to Berkeley, there is no such thing as matter. There is no external world. The things we ordinarily take to be material objects are nothing more than collections of ideas and have no existence outside of minds.

Consider the banana, again. What do we know about it? Well, it looks and feels to be a certain size and shape. It's firm and smooth to the touch. It looks yellow. It has a distinctive taste and smell. It makes a sound when we tap it or break its skin. In short, we know nothing about it apart from how it looks, sounds, feels, tastes, and smells. Our entire knowledge of it is limited to sensory ideas.

We assume, like Locke, that there is a material object causing these ideas. But Berkeley denied this. He said that there is nothing more to the banana than the ideas themselves. The banana *is* the ideas.

This doesn't mean that Berkeley denied the existence of bananas and other objects, it's just that he defined existence in a somewhat different fashion. He said that

to exist and to be perceived are actually the same thing. This is summed up by his famous phrase *esse* is *percipi*, a combination of Latin and English that means "to be is to be perceived."

the cause of our ideas

If material objects don't cause our ideas of the world, what does? Berkeley's answer was God.

When I look at a banana, God puts banana-colored and banana-shaped images into my mind. When I pick it up, He puts banana-type tactile impressions into my mind. When I smell it, he puts the characteristic banana smell into my mind. And so on.

If you happen to be looking at, touching, or smelling the same banana, that's because God is implanting banana-colored, banana-shaped, banana-feeling, banana-smelling ideas into your mind, too. Your ideas won't be identical to mine, since God provides you with your own viewpoint on the world. But, crucially, there is nothing more to the banana than the ideas in my mind, in your mind, and in the mind of God.

continued existence

If, as Berkeley claimed, "to be is to be perceived," doesn't that imply that objects are constantly popping into and out of existence?

I am alone in my office, right now. If I close the curtains, walk outside, and shut the door, does all of the furniture disappear? By Berkeley's account it seems that it must, since no one is perceiving it.

Berkeley said not. He said that the objects in the world have continuous existence because they are constantly perceived by at least one mind: the mind of God:

... all the choir of heaven and furniture of the earth, in a word all those bodies which compose the mighty frame of the world, have not any subsistence without a mind. Their being is to be perceived or known. Consequently so long as they are not actually perceived by me, or do not exist in my mind or that of any other created spirit, they must either have no existence at all, or else subsist in the mind of some eternal spirit.

God in the quad

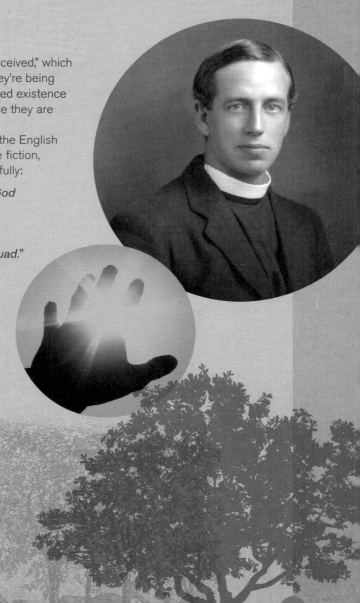

Berkeley claimed that "to be is to be perceived," which implies that objects don't exist *unless* they're being perceived. Nonetheless, objects' continued existence is guaranteed, Berkeley insisted, because they are continuously perceived by God.

A famous limerick, often attributed to the English priest, theologian, and writer of detective fiction, Ronald Knox, expresses this idea beautifully:

There was a young man who said, "God
Must think it exceedingly odd
If he finds that this tree
Continues to be
When there's no one about in the Quad."

REPLY
Dear Sir: Your astonishment's odd:
I am always about in the Quad.
And that's why the tree
Will continue to be,
Since observed by,
Yours faithfully, GOD.

what is ethics?

how to live

Ethics is the branch of philosophy concerned with values and human action. It seeks the answers to questions concerning good and bad, right and wrong, and the purpose and meaning of life.

The two biggest questions in ethics are, "What is the best way to live?" and "Which actions are right and which are wrong?"

not easy

Ethics is, in many respects, more practical and accessible than the other main branches of philosophy. Logic can seem technical and difficult to those not naturally drawn to mathematical and abstract thinking. Metaphysics can seem mysterious and abstruse. Epistemology can seem finicky and divorced from common sense. But ethics, dealing as it does with familiar subjects that matter in everyday life, has a more immediate and obvious appeal. That doesn't make it any less intellectually demanding than the other branches of philosophy, not when you get right down to it. In ethics—as in logic, metaphysics, and epistemology—ideas and viewpoints must be justified by argument and subjected to rigorous scrutiny.

Socrates's practical ethics

We have already seen, in chapter 1, that Socrates was the first to apply the philosophers' method of critical inquiry to questions about life and how best to live it. His interest in ethics wasn't merely theoretical. Far from it. He believed that the more knowledge and understanding we gain of ethical matters, the better and happier our lives will be.

One of his central claims was that once we truly understand what is good we will do it. In other words, all wrongdoing is ultimately grounded in ignorance of what constitutes the true good for ourselves and others.

That is why Socrates was so keen on debating such questions as, "What is courage?" and "What is justice?" and "What is temperance?" He believed that the more knowledge we gain of such things, the more courageous, just, and temperate we will become.

ethics as a way of life

This practical attitude toward ethics was shared by many early thinkers. The Greek philosopher Epicurus (341–270 BCE), for example, believed that the whole purpose of philosophy is to teach us to live happily and well. The aim of life is to achieve happiness, which, in practical terms, means experiencing pleasure and avoiding pain. In Epicurus' view:

It is impossible to live a pleasant life without living wisely and well and justly, and it is impossible to live wisely and well and justly without living pleasantly.

Zeno of Citium (ca. 335–ca. 263 BCE), a contemporary of Epicurus, also saw philosophy as a way of life. He founded the Stoic school of philosophy, which advocated the development of virtue, self-control, and fortitude in order to achieve a happy, untroubled state of mind.

A later Stoic, the Roman Emperor Marcus Aurelius (121–80 CE), summed up this approach to philosophy and life thus:

If you work at that which is before you, following right reason seriously, vigorously, calmly, without allowing anything else to distract you… If you hold to this, expecting nothing, but satisfied to live now according to nature, speaking heroic truth in every word that you utter, you will live happy. And there is no man able to prevent this.

a change of emphasis

These early thinkers, and others like them, were very much preoccupied with the first big question of ethics, "What is the best way to live?" But, as the centuries passed, the focus of ethics shifted in the direction of the second big question, "Which actions are right and which are wrong?"

It is this second question that will concern us most in this chapter. But we will begin by looking at two interesting and influential answers to the first question.

Epicurus on happiness

Epicurus advocated a life of simple pleasures, friendship, and retirement. He believed that the whole point of philosophy is to teach us to live happily and well, so ethics was, for him, a very practical matter—a way of life rather than a subject for intellectual speculation.

According to Epicurus, the aim of life is to experience pleasure—and as much of it as possible:

We maintain that pleasure is the beginning and end of a blessed life.

He felt little need to debate this since we all know and feel and experience the truth of it:

We recognize [pleasure] as our primary and natural good. Pleasure is our starting point whenever we choose or avoid anything, and it is this we make our aim, using feeling as the criterion by which we judge of every good thing.

what is meant by hedonism?

In philosophy, the view that pleasure is the primary good is known as "hedonism," from the Greek word *hedonikos*, meaning "pleasurable." Epicurus, then, was a hedonist, but only in the philosophical sense.

pleasures and pains

Nowadays, the word "hedonist" is generally used to label someone who indulges without restraint in sensual pleasures of every kind. But in that sense, Epicurus was the farthest thing from being a hedonist. Although he was convinced that pleasure is the highest good, he was equally convinced that pain is the worst of evils. So, for him, the avoidance of pain was every bit as important as the pursuit of pleasure, and this meant forgoing the kinds of pleasures that have harmful consequences.

Epicurus taught that is not enough simply to pursue pleasure, we must pursue it wisely. If we are driven by our impulses we will make wrong choices, sacrificing long-term well-being for short-term gratification. But if we are guided by reason, we will secure lasting happiness. He wrote:

When we say, then, that pleasure is the end and aim, we do not mean the pleasures of the prodigal or the pleasures

of sensuality… By pleasure we mean the absence of pain in the body and of trouble in the soul. It is not an unbroken succession of drinking bouts and of merrymaking…

Drinking bouts and merrymaking may sound like fun in the short term, but in the long run they lead to ill-health and mental distress. Therefore they are to be shunned.

tranquillity

A moment's reflection is enough to convince most of us of the dangers of gluttony, drunkenness, and the like, but, according to Epicurus, there are other, more subtle, snares that may entrap us.

For example, most of us take it for granted that wealth brings pleasure. Not so, declares Epicurus. On the contrary, the desire for riches makes us restless when we might be contented and anxious when we might be at peace. Once we open ourselves to avarice, no amount of wealth can satisfy our craving. Furthermore, we suffer constant anxiety in case we lose the wealth we already possess.

The pursuit of power and reputation is

the Garden… and beyond

In 306 BCE, Epicurus bought a house and some land outside Athens and set up his own very practical school, which became known as *Ho Kepos*, the Garden. This was a place where people from all walks of life could practice the self-sufficient, stress-free, contemplative lifestyle his philosophy advocated.

His influence extended way beyond his lifetime and way beyond the confines of the Garden. Epicurean societies flourished throughout the Hellenistic and the Roman world right up until the fourth century CE.

Aspects of Epicurus's philosophy have influenced some of history's greatest thinkers, including David Hume, Jeremy Bentham, Karl Marx, Arthur Schopenhauer, and Friedrich Nietzsche.

likewise attended with troubles. So Epicurus exhorted his followers to shun political and public life.

For Epicurus, the key concept is tranquillity. We maximize the pleasure in our lives not by rushing around in pursuit of one thrill after another or by piling up possessions but rather by learning to enjoy the simple things in life.

Aristotle on virtue

Aristotle, we now know, was interested in a wide range of philosophical questions. In ethics, he was particularly concerned with the question of what constitutes the good life. His ideas on this subject can be found in one of philosophy's most celebrated works, the *Nicomachean Ethics*.

Aristotle begins by arguing that the ultimate aim of human life is happiness. We all seek after many things—wealth, knowledge, friendship, reputation, and so on. Some of these things have intrinsic value, but at least part of our reason for seeking them is that we believe they will make us happy. The only thing we seek entirely for its own sake is happiness, therefore happiness is the supreme good.

But when Aristotle talks about happiness, he means more than just the feelings of pleasure and enjoyment. The word he uses is *eudaimonia*, a Greek word that is better translated as "well-being" or "flourishing." So, for Aristotle, happiness isn't just about feeling good, it's about flourishing.

an activity of the soul

Aristotle thought that all things in nature have goals, or purposes. For example, a rock's goal is simply to be at rest, a flower's goals include growing and blooming, and an animal's goals include reproducing and experiencing pleasure.

The distinctive goal of us humans, he said, is to fulfill our natures as rational beings. The happy or *eudaimon* life consists in achieving that goal.

Human happiness, then, involves making good use of our powers of reason. It requires us to conduct ourselves wisely and to respond to the changing circumstances of life in the right sorts of ways. It requires a sense of fulfillment, the feeling that we are doing something with our lives and making something of ourselves.

Happiness, for Aristotle, isn't a passive thing, it's active. It isn't something we *feel* or something we *have*. It's something we *do*. He famously defined happiness as "an activity of the soul in accordance with virtue."

virtue and the good life

By virtue, Aristotle means the disposition to behave in the right manner. In other words, the tendency to do the right thing, at the

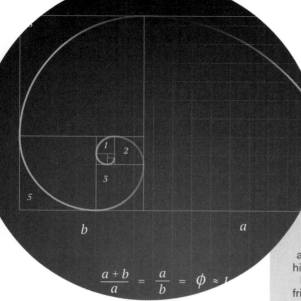

$$\frac{a+b}{a} = \frac{a}{b} = \phi \approx 1$$

the golden mean

Aristotle believed that balance is an essential element of the life well-lived.

If we examine any aspect of our lives, he said, we will find that there is a virtuous middle state lying between two nonvirtuous extremes. This middle state is often referred to as the golden mean, although Aristotle himself never used the phrase.

For example, we all have to face frightening situations from time to time. If we allow fear to overwhelm us and prevent us from acting decisively then we are *cowardly*, but if we are oblivious to fear and behave recklessly, then we are *foolhardy*. Between these two vices lies *courage*, a middle state in which we give fear its due but don't allow it to dictate our actions.

Similar considerations apply to anger. Those who take anger to excess are *wrathful*, whereas those deficient in anger are *timid*. Once again, the virtuous person steers a middle course. It is difficult to come up with an appropriate label, but *assertive* comes close.

It's important to note that the golden mean doesn't necessarily lie halfway between two extremes. Its precise location depends upon the individual and upon circumstances. For example, what would be considered courageous in a soldier might be considered foolhardy in a civilian.

right time, for the right purpose, and in the right sort of way.

So, the good life is a virtuous life. This means that we can only become happy, in the proper sense of the word, if we develop virtues such as courage, temperance, liberality, truthfulness, and the like.

There is, to be sure, an element of good fortune involved, too. Some external goods—health, wealth, education, and so forth—are necessary to us if we are to achieve our potential as rational beings. Events beyond our control can prevent even the wisest and best of us from flourishing. This means that virtue doesn't guarantee happiness, but happiness is impossible without it.

duty

Some philosophers claim that certain actions are unequivocally right or wrong. In other words, certain things, such as keeping promises, ought always to be done, and certain other things, such as stealing, ought never to be done.

By this account, we all have duties that we are obligated to perform. When we perform those duties we act rightly, and when we fail to perform those duties we act wrongly. In philosophy, this approach to ethics is known as "deontology," from the Greek *deon*, meaning "obligation" or "duty."

divine commands

The deontological approach to morality raises the obvious question of how we can know what those duties are. For millions of people all over the world the answer is equally obvious—we can know what our duties are because *God tells us* what they are.

A Christian, for example, might point to the Ten Commandments in the Old Testament or to Christ's command to love your neighbor as yourself as examples of unequivocal duties.

This response is open to a number of objections. What reason do we have for believing that those really are God's commands? Why should we place so much trust in the Bible? Is it reasonable to believe that God exists and that He is sufficiently wise and benevolent to have the last word on moral matters?

These are interesting and important questions, but for our present purposes we'll lay them aside and consider another objection, which will have a familiar ring.

Euthyphro revisited

In chapter 1, we examined a portion of Plato's dialogue the *Euthyphro*, in which Socrates discusses holiness with a priest named Euthyphro.

At one point, Euthyphro tries to define holiness by saying:

The holy is what all the gods love.

Socrates responds with what has become known as the *Euthyphro* dilemma:

> **Is the holy loved by the gods because it is holy? Or is it holy because it is loved by the gods?**

In a modified form—"Is what is morally good commanded by God because it is morally good, or is it morally good because it is commanded by God?"—the Euthyphro dilemma presents a challenge to anyone who tries to define right and wrong in terms of God's commands.

On the one hand, if God commands/prohibits certain actions because they are good/bad in themselves, then morality is independent of God. He may, through his great wisdom and power, have a role to play in explaining or enforcing the moral code, but He doesn't create it. In fact, He is just as much subject to it as we are.

In that case, God is not, strictly speaking, necessary to morality. Furthermore, merely knowing that He approves or disapproves of certain things doesn't help us to understand what it is that makes them good or bad.

On the other hand, if right/wrong actions are simply those that God commands/prohibits, then to say that God is good or that God's commands are good tells us

nothing very meaningful about either God or His commands. "God is good" simply means "God does those things which God commands;" and "God's commands are good" simply means "God's commands are God's commands."

In this case, morality is an arbitrary affair. If God were to command the torture of puppies then torturing puppies would be morally good.

picking and choosing

There is a practical difficulty connected with the view that morality is about performing duties revealed to us by God.

Consider this commandment from the book of Exodus in the Bible:

> *Six days shall work be done, but on the seventh day there shall be to you an holy day, a Sabbath of rest to the LORD: whosoever doeth work therein shall be put to death.*

There are few believers today who obey God's command to put Sabbath-day workers to death. But why?

Believers typically find ways to explain away the duty to obey commands of this kind, but in deciding which commandments are still binding and which need explaining away, aren't they, in fact, having to rely upon *their own* moral intuitions?

Most believers, when presented with the *Euthyphro* dilemma, plump for the option that God commands/prohibits certain actions because they are good/bad in themselves. But this is to concede that the moral code is ultimately independent of God and still requires explanation.

Kant and the categorical imperative

The German philosopher Immanuel Kant (1724–1804) is one of the most important philosophers of all time. His brilliant and original contributions to epistemology, metaphysics, and ethics have had a major influence on all subsequent philosophy. Kant brought about a revolution in epistemology and metaphysics by effecting a synthesis between the two competing philosophies of his time, empiricism and rationalism (discussed in chapter 3). He argued that the empiricists were wrong in maintaining that the mind is a blank slate until marked by the pen of experience and claimed that the rationalists were mistaken in maintaining that a priori knowledge of the world outside the mind is possible.

a monotonous life

Kant's thinking was bold and adventurous, but his lifestyle wasn't. He spent his entire life in the town of Königsberg in East Prussia (now Kaliningrad in Russia), where for many years he worked as a private tutor before obtaining the chair in logic and metaphysics at the university, in 1770.

His habits were so regular and punctual that his neighbors are said to have set their clocks by his afternoon walks. He never married, rarely traveled far from his hometown, and wasn't fond of socializing. He suffered from fragile health, but his lifestyle was so strict and moderate that he lived to be 80. Despite his provincial, staid, and reclusive lifestyle, he was an intellectual firebrand.

Kant's ethics

Kant's ethical ideas were no less influential than his ideas in epistemology and metaphysics. His approach was deontological. He claimed that acting morally is a matter of performing certain duties, which are binding to everyone in all circumstances. Although he was a devout Christian, rather than look to the Bible to discover these duties he looked to reason. He claimed that every rational person can see what our moral duties are simply by giving the matter some careful thought and that any reasonable person can understand that an action can only be considered right if it is based upon a maxim that can be universalized. It is wrong to act in accordance with rules or principles that couldn't be adopted by everyone.

the categorical imperative

Kant argued that our moral duty can be summed up in one rule:

what are maxims and the universalizability test?

In everyday language, maxims are simple rules or guides for living. Two familiar examples are, "live hard, die young" and "one good turn deserves another." But Kant uses the term in a more technical sense to refer to the subjective principles, or intentions, that guide a person's actions.

For example, someone who receives too much change from a shopkeeper and decides to keep it might be acting upon the maxim "to increase my wealth by any safe means."

Kant argued that the moral worth of an action can be judged according to its underlying maxim. If it's a maxim that can be universalized—that is, if everyone could adopt it—then the action is morally acceptable. But if it's one that can't be universalized, then the action is morally unacceptable.

Suppose I decided to make my living by burglary. In this case, I would be acting upon the maxim "get all the things I need by stealing from others." But, however selfish and unsavory a character I might be, I am capable, as a rational being, of understanding that this principle cannot be universalized, because if everybody were to adopt it nobody would produce anything, and there would be nothing to steal.

My maxim is impossible to universalize; therefore, in acting upon it, I act wrongly. Furthermore, as a rational being, I can *see* that I act wrongly.

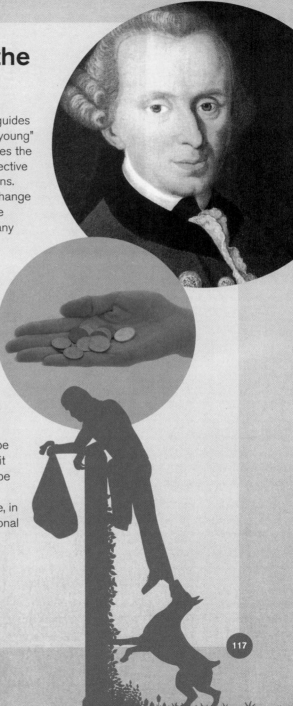

ends not means

Although Kant held that there is only one categorical imperative, he formulated it in a number of different ways. The version we have already discussed, he labeled "the formula of the universal law."

An alternative version, which Kant called "the formula of the end in itself," is:

> *Act in such a way that you always treat humanity, whether in your own person or in the person of any other, never simply as a means, but always at the same time as an end.*

In this version, he stresses the importance of respecting everyone's rights, as rational beings, to make free choices of their own. This means that we should never treat other people merely as objects that can be manipulated and used for our own ends but must instead treat them as self-determining beings. It is always wrong to coerce, deceive, or in any way manipulate another person as a means of getting what we want. We can cooperate with them or strike bargains with them, but we mustn't *use* them. They're not there for our convenience; they are valuable in themselves.

last words

Although Kant was a first-rate philosopher, he wasn't much of a writer. Such works as the *Critique of Pure Reason* and the *Groundwork of the Metaphysics of Morals* contain the most profound philosophy, but they are couched in horribly difficult and unnecessarily technical language.

His last words—"*Es ist gut*"—however, were a model of profundity and simplicity. They translate as, "It is good."

The words on his tomb, "the starry heav d from Kant's own writings. The full quote, from the *Critique of Practical Reason*, reads:

> *Two things fill the mind with ever-increasing wonder and awe, the more often and the more intensely the mind of thought is drawn to them: the starry heavens above me and the moral law within me.*

Act only according to that maxim whereby you can at the same time will that it should become a universal law without contradiction.

This he called the categorical imperative. It is *categorical* because it is absolute and unqualified, applying at all times and in all circumstances, and it is *imperative* because it expresses a command.

Any morally significant action can be tested by the categorical imperative. For example, I might wonder whether it's morally acceptable for me to spend some time each day kicking back and relaxing. So I ask myself whether I, as a rational and benevolent being, would be happy for *everyone* to do that. The answer is yes, so it's OK. However, I might wonder if it's OK for me to kick back and relax permanently and live on state handouts. So I ask myself whether I, as a rational and benevolent being, would be happy for *everyone* to do that. The answer is, no, it wouldn't work, so it's not OK.

what about feelings or consequences?

For Kant, morality isn't about feelings. It is about recognizing and doing one's duty.

I may have feelings of compassion that prompt me to volunteer at a soup kitchen or donate money to an animal shelter. At the same time, I may feel perfectly OK about stealing stationery from my workplace or telling lies to get myself out of trouble. For Kant, feelings are not the issue. What matters, morally, is that I recognize and do my duty, whatever I feel about it.

Morality is not about consequences. Once I have recognized a duty, I am morally obligated to perform it whatever the circumstances and whatever the consequences. It might, perhaps, sometimes be convenient to lie, but we cannot reasonably wish that everyone tell lies when it's convenient, so we have a moral duty not to lie. We ought to perform this duty, Kant claims, even if it's likely to result in bad consequences. In an essay entitled *On a Supposed Right to Lie on Altruistic Motives*, he even goes so far as to say that we would be morally obligated not to lie to a would-be murderer about the whereabouts of his intended victim.

Our moral responsibility only extends to those things that are directly under the control of our rational wills, says Kant, so morality is about intentions rather than feelings or consequences. We might not be able to control how we *feel* about doing our duty. We might not be able to foresee or control the *consequences* of doing it. But we can control our *intentions*. We can always choose to act, insofar as circumstances allow, in accordance with our duty.

consequences

Previously, we examined the deontological approach to ethics, according to which there are certain things that are unequivocally right or wrong and which we categorically ought or ought not to do. It will come as no surprise to readers to learn that many philosophers reject this view and insist that it is not actions in themselves but rather their outcomes that are important from a moral standpoint. This approach to ethics is known as "consequentialism."

Consequentialists claim that actions ought to be considered right or wrong not according to their conformity with absolute rules but according to whether they bring about good or bad results. An action is right if it has good consequences and wrong if it has bad consequences. No type of action is inherently wrong.

no absolute duties

Take lying. The deontologist claims that lying is always wrong and that we ought never to do it. But the consequentialist retorts, "What *makes* it wrong?" The answer must be that it leads, or has a tendency to lead, to some undesirable state of affairs. But, this being the case, the problem isn't really the lying, it's the consequences.

So, on those occasions when lying leads to a desirable state of affairs, it makes no sense to refrain from doing it merely out of some misplaced sense of duty.

By this account, telling a lie to put a would-be murderer off the trail of his intended victim would—except in very strange and unusual circumstances—be considered a right action, since it helps to protect a life. Similarly, torturing someone might be considered morally acceptable if it helps to prevent a terrorist attack or to uncover a pedophile ring.

what is good?

Consequentialists argue that the more good an action produces, the better it is. So, in any given set of circumstances, the best action is the one that produces the most good.

But what criteria should be used to judge the outcomes of actions? It's all very well to say that actions are right insofar as their consequences are good, but what do we mean by good?

There are many things that we humans consider to be good—love, truth, justice,

experiencing pleasure or avoiding pain and that pleasure is therefore the only thing that is good in itself.

In his own words: "Nature has placed mankind under the governance of two sovereign masters, pain and pleasure. It is for them alone to point out what we ought to do, as well as to determine what we shall do."

freedom, knowledge, friendship, and artistic achievement, to name just a few. So we might consider actions good insofar as they promote any of those things.

happiness: the ultimate good

However, the English philosopher and social reformer Jeremy Bentham (see page 122) insisted that there is just one human good—happiness. He claimed that actions are good insofar as they lead to an increase in happiness, and are bad insofar as they lead to a decrease in happiness. But this raises the further question of what happiness is.

In answering this question, Bentham took his cue from Epicurus (see page 110) and identified happiness with pleasure. He said that all human activity is directed toward

ideal utilitarianism

The English philosopher G. E. Moore (1873–1958) disagreed with Bentham's claim that pleasure is the only good. He argued that there are other things— ideals, such as beauty, friendship, justice, and compassion—which are good independently of, and even in the absence of, any pleasure they might bring.

Moore was a consequentialist. But, unlike Bentham, he didn't think that actions should be judged solely in terms of how much pleasure they produce. He thought that the extent to which they promoted those other goods was important, too. His version of consequentialism is known as "ideal utilitarianism."

Bentham & happiness

Jeremy Bentham (1748–1832) is regarded as the father of modern utilitarianism. The cornerstone of his philosophy is "the principle of utility," more commonly known as the "greatest happiness principle."

Bentham's particular brand of consequentialism was built upon the premise that actions are good insofar as they promote pleasure or happiness and bad insofar as they lead to pain or unhappiness. This raises the question of whose pleasure and happiness we are talking about. Bentham's answer was *everyone's*. Furthermore, he believed that everyone has an equal right to happiness, regardless of race, gender, or social status.

utilitarianism and the greatest happiness principle

Bentham claimed that actions can be considered good or bad, right or wrong, according to the contribution they make to the sum total of human happiness. This theory is known as "utilitarianism." It is by far the most important and influential consequentialist ethical theory.

At the heart of utilitarianism is Bentham's greatest happiness principle, which states that, in any situation, the morally correct action is the one that brings the greatest happiness to the greatest number of people.

To see how this works, take the example of a wealthy factory owner who would like to increase his wealth by reducing his workers' wages. Would he be morally justified in doing this? Well, cutting salaries would lead to a small increase in his own happiness, and perhaps that of his family and friends, but it would decrease the happiness of his many employees. It doesn't lead to the greatest happiness of the greatest number—far from it. Therefore, according to the greatest happiness principle, he ought not to do it.

In the real world, things are not always so clear-cut. It can be difficult to judge the effect an action is likely to have on the happiness of those it affects. Bentham realized this, and proposed a "felicific calculus," a method of calculating the quantity of pleasure likely to result from an act.

the felicific calculus

According to utilitarianism, the ultimate aim of our moral endeavors is to bring the greatest happiness to the greatest number. But how is this possible? How can we determine—or even estimate—the amount of happiness that will result from a given course of action?

Bentham's solution to this problem was his felicific calculus—an algorithm for quantifying pleasures and for calculating their sum total for any given course of action and for all parties concerned. It took account of several factors:

Intensity of pleasure
Duration of pleasure
Certainty of pleasure (the probability that it will occur)
Propinquity of pleasure (how soon it will occur)
Fecundity: the likelihood that the action will lead to further pleasures later
Purity: the likelihood that the action won't lead to pains later
Extent: the number of people that the action will affect

The felicific calculus is difficult to remember, let alone apply, so Bentham offered the following mnemonic rhyme, encapsulating its principles in a user-friendly form:

Intense, long, certain, speedy, fruitful, pure—
Such marks in pleasures and in pains endure.
Such pleasures seek if private be thy end:
If it be public, wide let them extend
Such pains avoid, whichever be thy view:
If pains must come, let them extend to few.

123

rule-utilitarianism

A common criticism of utilitarianism is that it's impractical. It just isn't possible to perform a series of calculations every time we're faced with a moral decision. We need rules and guidelines to simplify and speed up the process.

Another criticism of utilitarianism is that it has some strange and troubling implications. In the words of the American philosopher Richard B. Brandt (1910–97):

> *It implies that if you have employed a boy to mow your lawn and he has finished the job and asks for his pay, you should pay him what you have promised only if you cannot find a better use for your money. It implies that when you bring home your monthly paycheck you should use it to support your family and yourself only if it cannot be used more effectively to supply the needs of others.*

These problems have led some philosophers, notably Brandt himself, to propose a modified form of utilitarianism, which goes by the name of "rule-utilitarianism."

The standard form of utilitarianism, which we can label "act-utilitarianism," applies the greatest happiness principle to individual acts. Rule-utilitarianism, on the other hand, applies the greatest happiness principle to moral rules. It seeks to discover general rules and guidelines which, if adopted by everyone, will lead to the greatest good. Such rules might include paying people what you promise to pay them, and using your paycheck first and foremost to support your family and yourself.

According to act-utilitarianism, an action is right if it produces the greatest good, whereas according to rule-utilitarianism, an action is right if it conforms to a rule that leads to the greatest good.

higher and lower pleasures

According to Bentham, the quantity of a pleasure, its intensity and duration, is important. But the nature of a pleasure—whether it comes from eating oysters, listening to Beethoven, or reading trashy novels—is irrelevant. No pleasure is intrinsically superior to any other. "The quantity of pleasure being equal, push-pin [a child's game] is as good as poetry," he said.

The 19th-century philosopher and social reformer John Stuart Mill (1806–73) disagreed. His father was a close friend and ally of Jeremy Bentham. Under their influence, Mill became a strong advocate of utilitarianism, but he didn't accept all of Bentham's views and argued that some pleasures *are* intrinsically superior to others.

He distinguished between what he called higher and lower pleasures. Lower pleasures, such as eating, drinking, and sex, are those that appeal to our animal nature. Higher pleasures, such as friendship, art, poetry, and philosophy, are those that appeal to our higher, nobler human capacities.

Mill insisted that anyone who has experienced higher pleasures knows that they are superior to lower ones and will prefer them even if they don't result in a greater quantity of pleasure. He wrote:

> Few human creatures would consent to be changed into any of the lower animals for a promise of the fullest allowance of a beast's pleasures; no intelligent human being would consent to be a fool, no instructed person would be an ignoramus, no person of feeling and conscience would be selfish and base, even though they should be persuaded that the fool, the dunce, or the rascal is better satisfied with his lot than they are with theirs.

Jeremy Bentham: reformist

Bentham qualified as a lawyer but never practiced law, as his interests lay in the wider field of legal reform. He believed legislators of his time were too much influenced by what he called the "principle of sympathy and antipathy," which meant punishing things they disliked, regardless of whether they did any actual harm, and condoning things they approved of without regard for any suffering they might cause. He wanted to reform the legal system so that it was based instead on what he called the "principle of utility," which approves or disapproves of actions according to their tendency to augment or diminish happiness.

He was a freethinker, a political radical, and an advocate of individual freedoms. Politically active in the late 18th and early 19th centuries, he was far ahead of his time, championing the abolition of slavery, equal rights for women, decriminalization of homosexual acts, abolition of the death penalty, animal welfare, and the abolition of physical punishment.

applied ethics

Applied ethics is practical ethics. It looks at how ethical principles apply to real-world morally contentious situations.

Ethics can be divided into three sub-branches: normative ethics, applied ethics, and metaethics. So far we have focused on normative ethics (meaning "establishing, or deriving from, a standard or norm"), which seeks to discover the moral principles that dictate how we ought to live. Applied ethics investigates how moral principles can be applied to specific issues such as animal rights or abortion. And metaethics is concerned with questions about the nature of ethics itself. Here we will look at an issue from applied ethics, that of whether animals are entitled to moral consideration.

animals and ethics

Even ethicists as diverse from one another as Kant and Bentham could agree that human beings ought always to be treated with consideration and respect. Kant's categorical imperative states that we should always treat people as ends in themselves and never merely as means to an end. And Bentham insisted that when considering the distribution of happiness, every person's interests count equally.

But what about animals? Should we treat them with consideration and respect, too, or are we at liberty to use them as we wish?

no moral status

Until the latter part of the 18th century, Western philosophers had little to say in support of animal welfare. Those philosophers who considered the subject at all tended to agree that human beings have few if any moral obligations toward them.

Aristotle, for example, took it as a fundamental principle of justice that "equals should be treated equally and unequals unequally." Animals, he argued, are beneath us, since they cannot reason. Therefore we are justified in treating them unequally. We can use them as mere conveniences.

Thomas Aquinas, unsurprisingly, agreed with Aristotle, saying that since animals are instinctual whereas humans engage in rational thought, animals have a lower moral status. We need have no qualms about eating them or using them, because that's what they were created for: "[T]he life of animals and plants is preserved not for themselves but for man... by a most just ordinance of the Creator, both their life and their death are subject to our use."

Descartes had even less sympathy, claiming that animals, unlike humans, have no souls. They are nothing more than complex biological automatons with no real thoughts or feelings and thus have no moral status and require no consideration at all.

Kant, too, held that animals have no claim to moral consideration, arguing that only rational beings with enough self-awareness to reflect on their own desires and impulses have moral status and should be considered ends in themselves. This sets people "infinitely above all the other beings on earth… with which one may deal and dispose at one's discretion."

animal rights

All these thinkers shared the view that something sets us apart from animals and entitles us, but not them, to moral consideration.

Jeremy Bentham, who is generally credited with being the first major thinker to support animal rights, disagreed. He said that the question of whether animals can reason or not is beside the point. Animals differ from us in many ways—number of legs, type of skin, shape, size—but these things no more justify us in mistreating them than the color of a man's skin justifies us in mistreating him. And the same applies to animals' inability to reason. The only thing that matters, ethically, is something that we and many animals have in common—the capacity to suffer. In his *Introduction to the Principles of Morals and Legislation*, he wrote:

The question is not, Can they reason? nor, Can they talk? but, Can they suffer? Why should the law refuse its protection to any sensitive being? The time will come when humanity will extend its mantle over everything which breathes...

animal liberation

The contemporary Australian philosopher Peter Singer's 1975 book *Animal Liberation* is widely credited with igniting the modern animal-rights movement.

In it, Singer extends Bentham's greatest happiness principle—"the greatest good of the greatest number"—to certain animals as well as humans. Like Bentham, he argues that all beings capable of suffering deserve moral consideration.

metaethics

Metaethics is the branch of ethics concerned with questions about the nature of ethical properties, attitudes, statements, and judgments.

In ethics, questions such as "What is the best way to live?" and "Which actions are right and which are wrong?" are known as "first-order questions." These are practical questions that require practical answers. That is, answers which serve as guides to how we ought to act. Normative ethics and applied ethics are concerned with questions of this type.

Ethicists are also interested in another set of questions, known as "second-order questions." These aren't practical questions about what we should or shouldn't do but rather questions about the actual nature of ethics. Examples of second-order questions include, "Where do moral values come from?" and "What do people mean when they use words such as 'right' and 'wrong'?" and "Are moral values absolute, or does morality vary according to time, place, and culture?" The branch of ethics that explores questions of this kind is called "metaethics."

are there universal moral values?

The central problem in metaethics concerns the status of moral values and whether they are objective and universal or merely relative, a matter of culture and preference.

Moral realism is the view that there are objective moral facts. Certain states of affairs really are good, while others really are bad. Similarly, certain actions really are right, while others really are wrong. The task of ethics is to discover moral facts not to decide upon them.

If moral realism is correct then statements such as "we shouldn't cause unnecessary suffering to animals" and "stealing is wrong" are genuinely meaningful ones, which can be true or false and which can be rationally investigated and debated.

Moral relativism is the theory that moral values are relative. There are no objective facts about what is good or bad, right or wrong, only preferences and opinions.

the is–ought problem

David Hume rejected moral realism. One of his reasons for doing so was that he noticed a troubling logical gap between facts and values.

In *A Treatise of Human Nature*, he wrote:

In every system of morality, which I have hitherto met with, I have always remark'd, that the author proceeds for some time in the ordinary ways of reasoning, and establishes the being of a God, or makes observations concerning human affairs; when all of a sudden I am surpriz'd to find, that instead of the usual copulations of propositions, is, and is not, I meet with no proposition that is not connected with an ought, or an ought not. This change is imperceptible; but is however, of the last consequence. For as this ought, or ought not, expresses some new relation or affirmation, 'tis necessary that it shou'd be observ'd and explain'd; and at the same time that a reason should be given; for what seems altogether inconceivable, how this new relation can be a deduction from others, which are entirely different from it.

In other words, he accuses moral philosophers of making invalid inferences from propositions concerning facts to propositions concerning values. The trouble is that facts and values are fundamentally different sorts of things. You can't make the logical leap from propositions of the one type to propositions of the other.

an example
A nonvegetarian might argue:

The fact that humans have canine teeth shows that meat is a natural part of our diet.
Therefore it's OK for humans to eat meat.

Notice the move from descriptive statements—"humans have canine teeth" and "meat is a natural part of our diet"—to an evaluative conclusion that "it's OK for humans to eat meat." According to Hume, you can't derive an ought from an is, in this manner. At least, not without further argument.

Different cultures hold different beliefs about what is good and bad and what is right and wrong. It could be argued that this is because ethics is not yet an exact science. People are still grasping after moral truths. But moral relativists take a different line. They say that moral disagreement occurs because are no universal moral truths to *be* grasped. By this account, morality is nothing more than a description of the practices and norms adopted by specific social groups at specific places and times. Slavery was right and good for certain societies in the past but wrong and bad for most modern societies.

Moral relativism makes rational debate about moral values impossible, since there are no objective criteria by which they can be judged.

naturalism and the naturalistic fallacy

In ethics, naturalism is the theory that ethical terms can be derived from nonethical ones. According to the ethical naturalist, theories about what is good or bad, right or wrong, can be based upon scientifically discoverable properties of the natural world.

For example, utilitarianism is a naturalistic ethical theory. It evaluates the rightness or wrongness of actions according to the total amount of pleasure or happiness they produce.

Naturalistic ethical theories seem to offer a way around the is–ought problem. If we define what is good, or right, in terms of a natural property, then we seem able to deduce evaluative propositions from factual ones. For example, a utilitarian might argue:

An action is good, or right, if it produces the greatest happiness for the greatest number.
In a given set of circumstances, action X produces the greatest happiness for the greatest number.
Therefore X is the good, or right, thing to do.

And the utilitarian appears to have successfully derived an ought from an is.

But antinaturalists point to a weakness in this line of reasoning, the naturalistic fallacy, a term coined by the English philosopher G. E. Moore (see page 121).

The naturalistic fallacy is committed whenever anyone tries to define an evaluative concept in terms of descriptive ones. To demonstrate that such definitions are invalid, Moore put forward what is called the open question argument.

To understand how the open question argument works, begin by considering a perfectly valid definition, such as "a bachelor is an unmarried man." In this case, given that George is a man and that he is unmarried, the question, "Is George a bachelor?" is a closed one. The answer is yes, and there is nothing more to be said. It would be absurd to say, "Yes, George is an unmarried man, but is he a bachelor?"

Next, consider what the antinaturalist would consider an invalid definition, such as "a good, or right, action is one that produces the greatest happiness for the greatest number." In this case, given that action X produces the greatest happiness for the greatest number, there should be no room for debate about whether it's the right thing to do. But, on the contrary, it remains an open question. We can always say, "Yes, X produces the greatest happiness, but is it the *right* thing to do?"

This shows that the original definition failed to capture the essence of what is good, or right. Moore argued that any attempt to define evaluative concepts from factual ones will always fall at precisely the same hurdle. It will always succumb to the open question argument.

Hume's treatise

Read Book III, Part I, Section I of David Hume's *Treatise of Human Nature* to gain a deeper insight into the is–ought problem. Better still, read the entire treatise. Hume is a philosopher and writer of the first rank and a pleasure to read.

philosophy of religion

the case for God

St. Thomas Aquinas

the case against God

the case for God

The philosophy of religion is concerned with two kinds of questions: 1) metaphysical questions regarding the nature and existence of God; and 2) epistemological questions relating to religious faith and experience. In this chapter, we will limit ourselves to a discussion of questions of the first kind.

Questions about the nature and existence of God are of more than speculative interest. We all have opinions about God, and most of us, from the most ardent believers to the most hardened atheists, have opinions that matter to us. Our attitude toward God shapes, in sometimes profound and important ways, the way we act, the way we think, the way we view the world, and our attitude to life itself.

theism

In the main, Western philosophers from the medieval period onward have tended to focus their attention upon a theistic conception of God. Theism is the belief that there is one God, the Creator and ruler of all things, unlimited in knowledge and power, supremely benevolent, transcendent and yet immanent in the world. This is the view of God taken by most Christians, Jews, and Muslims.

One of the most interesting things about this conception of God is that an argument can be made that such a being necessarily exists. This is the ontological argument which we have previously examined in chapter 4 on metaphysics. It is a fascinating argument, one which has generated an immense amount of philosophical debate over the past thousand or so years but is too abstract and metaphysical to hold much interest for the man or woman in the street. Very few people base a practical belief in God on the persuasiveness of the ontological argument.

In this section, we will examine two theistic arguments that have more practical appeal—by which I mean that, in addition to their philosophical interest, they have some persuasive power.

the design argument

The most popular and most persuasive argument for the existence of God is the design argument, which also goes by the somewhat fancier title, the teleological argument (from the Greek *telos*, meaning "purpose"). This argument has been around for a long time—there's even a version of it in the Bible: "The heavens declare the glory of God; and the firmament sheweth his handiwork" (Psalm 3:5).

Perhaps the best-known—and certainly one of the most engaging—expositions of the design argument comes from the 1802 work *Natural Theology or Evidences of the Existence and Attributes of the Deity* by the English clergyman, William Paley (1743–1805). It runs along the following lines.

Imagine you were walking across some moorland one day, and you chanced to hit your foot against a stone. Then suppose you were to pick up the stone, examine it, and ask yourself how it came to be there. Chances are, you wouldn't have much idea. For all you know, the stone might have been there since that part of the world was formed. Now, imagine you were walking across the same moorland one day, and you happened to stumble across a pocketwatch. Then suppose you were to pick up the pocketwatch, examine it, and ask yourself how it came to be there. In this case, your thoughts would be very different. You would hardly suppose that the pocketwatch might have been there indefinitely. You would see that it is an intricate piece of machinery, composed

he/she/it

God is generally regarded as sexless—as being incorporeal, in fact. In philosophical discussions, however, God has traditionally been referred to by the masculine pronoun.

Personally, I dislike referring to God as He. It seems to promote an idea of God that is both sexist and anthropocentric. Unfortunately, the alternatives, referring to God as She or It, are no better. Throughout this book, for want of a better alternative, I have stuck to the traditional masculine pronoun. But it isn't my intention to imply that God—if He/She/It exists—possesses either male or human characteristics.

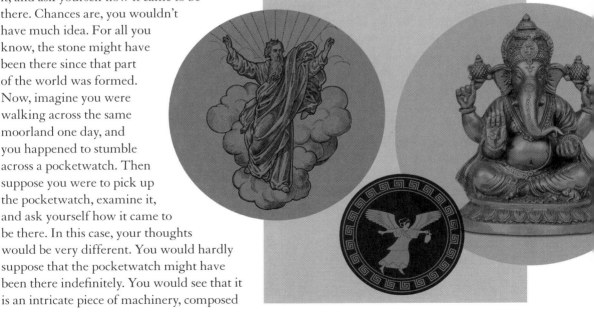

of cogs and springs and gears all perfectly fashioned and aligned for the purpose of telling the time. So you would assume that it must have been manufactured somewhere by a skilled craftsman. Even if you had never seen a pocketwatch before, and didn't fully understand its purpose, it would still be evident to you that it bears marks of design.

Precisely the same kind of reasoning, Paley argues, should convince us that the world has a designer.

The precise movements of the planets in their orbits, the teeming variety of animal and plant life, the symmetry and beauty of the rainbow, the complexity and fitness-for-purpose of organs such as the human eye—these and countless other natural wonders are clear evidence of divine handiwork.

Paley writes:

Every indication of contrivance, every manifestation of design, which existed in the watch, exists in the works of nature; with the difference, on the side of nature, of being greater and more, and that in a degree which exceeds all computation.

The essence of the design argument, then, is that the world bears unmistakable marks of design and that this is clear evidence of a designer. Furthermore, since the world is indescribably complex, it must have been designed and created by a being of unimaginable intelligence and power—that is, by God.

the first-cause argument

Another major argument for the existence of God is the first-cause argument, also known as the cosmological argument (from the Greek word *kosmos*, meaning "world"). This begins with the uncontroversial premise that the world exists. But, the argument continues, nothing springs into existence out of nothing. Everything that exists was caused to exist by something else prior to it. And this "something else" was itself caused to exist by some prior cause. But this chain of causes can't go back forever. There must have been a first cause. And that first cause is God.

The first-cause argument is closely associated with the medieval theologian and philosopher Thomas Aquinas (see page 138), who based it upon some arguments originally put forward by Aristotle. Aquinas was careful to stress that the first cause must be a being of a very different kind than every other being in the universe. It must be an uncaused cause. It must be the source of its own being. Were this not the case, the first-cause argument would be vulnerable to that most childish but vexing of objections, "But who made God?"

the first mover

In a short section of his vast work, the *Summa Theologica*, Aquinas offers five proofs of the existence of God. Three of these, the unmoved mover, the first cause (see page 136), and the argument from contingency are really just variations on a theme.

His unmoved argument runs along the following lines:

We can see just by looking around us that some things in the world are moving. But anything that is moving must have been moved by something else. Nothing just spontaneously moves.

Furthermore, the thing that moves another thing must itself be in motion. This means that it too must have been moved by something else. And so on, and so on. But this can't go on forever. There must have been a first mover. And that first mover is God.

Notice that Aquinas doesn't begin his argument by claiming that everything in the world is moving. Only that some things in the world are moving. So this argument isn't vulnerable to the objection, "But what moved God?", since God isn't moving. He is an unmoved mover.

St. Thomas Aquinas

Thomas Aquinas (1225–74) is considered by the Catholic Church to be her greatest-ever theologian. He was also perhaps the greatest of the medieval philosophers.

Thomas Aquinas was born in Aquino, Italy. At 14, he went to study philosophy and liberal arts at the University of Naples. His talent for learning was so remarkable that he is said to have quickly outstripped his teachers.

While in Naples he began to read the works of Aristotle, whose ideas were to have a lasting influence upon him. After completing his studies, Aquinas entered the Dominican Order of monks. His family opposed this, feeling that it was beneath their son's dignity to join what was then a newfangled monastic order—and, even worse, one that practiced poverty. Their opposition was so strong that two of his brothers had him imprisoned in the fortress of San Giovanni. They sent a prostitute into his room, hoping that her charms would weaken his religious resolve. Aquinas is said to have taken a burning brand from the fire and chased her from the room.

Soon afterward, Aquinas was released. He rejoined the Dominicans and spent the rest of his life among them. At first his fellow monks underestimated his talents, misled by his large girth and quiet disposition into thinking that he was slow-witted, and nicknaming him the "dumb ox." But they soon came to appreciate his intellectual gifts.

faith and reason

Aquinas's great ambition was to show that faith and reason needn't be enemies. He believed that God reveals His truth through both faculties. For example, we can know that God exists by placing faith in the teachings of the Church, but we can also know that God exists by mental assent to various philosophical arguments.

Aquinas's best-known philosophical work is the *Summa Theologica*, a comprehensive summary of Christian theology and philosophy. It is an enormous and complex work of over 3,000 "articles," each of which poses a particular question, such as "What is eternity?" or "Is it self-evident that God exists?" His responses examine the various arguments and counterarguments in meticulous detail.

Shortly after his death, Aquinas was canonized by Pope John XXII. His reputation continued to increase during the centuries that followed, so much so that in the late 19th century, Pope Leo XIII effectively made the theology of St. Thomas Aquinas the official theology of the Roman Catholic Church.

Aquinas and Aristotle

One of Aquinas's most notable contributions to medieval philosophy was his synthesis of Aristotelianism and Christianity.

Before Aquinas, Aristotle's ideas had been largely neglected in the West, but Aquinas brought them to the forefront of Roman Catholic doctrine and Western culture. Unfortunately, he was rather too zealous and successful in promoting the ideas and arguments of his favorite philosopher, and for the next 400 years, Aristotelianism dominated Western thought to such an extent that many scholars accepted Aristotle's opinions without question, sticking to them even when presented with evidence that contradicted them.

It wasn't until the 17th century and the emergence of scientifically minded thinkers, such as Francis Bacon and René Descartes, that philosophy was freed from this Aristotelian stranglehold.

the Five Ways

Aquinas also bequeathed to philosophy his celebrated Five Ways of proving the existence of God. The First, Second, and Third Ways are all variations of the cosmological argument (see page 136). In the Fourth Way, Aquinas observes that we judge some things to be better or worse than others: "Among beings there are some more and some less good, true, noble, and the like."

He then argues (not at all clearly or convincingly, or even comprehensibly) that to explain the existence of this gradation in being there must be some ultimate and perfect being: God.

The Fifth Way is a version of the design argument. Aquinas begins by saying that natural bodies, although they lack intelligence, always operate toward some end or purpose, and that it is evident that this happens not by chance but by design. He continues: "Now whatever lacks intelligence cannot move towards an end, unless it be directed by some being endowed with knowledge and intelligence; as the arrow is shot to its mark by the archer. Therefore some intelligent being exists by whom all natural things are directed to their end; and this being we call God."

the case against God

In the first section of this chapter we looked at two of the main philosophical arguments for the existence of God: the first-cause argument and the design argument. In this section, we will first look at some objections to these arguments, and we will also examine an important argument for the *non*existence of God.

The first-cause argument runs as follows. Everything has a cause; nothing springs into existence out of nothing. Since we know that the universe exists, there must be a chain of causes going back in time to account for its existence. But this chain of causes can't extend backward to infinity. There has to be a first cause: God.

One objection to this argument is that it contradicts itself. It begins by stating that everything has a cause but ends by saying that there is something which has no cause. Aquinas foresaw this objection, which is why he took pains to stress that the first cause must be a being of a very different kind from all of the other beings in the universe. The thought here is that God has a special status. He stands outside the universe and is not subject to the normal rules of causation.

But this is to concede that something *can* exist without a prior cause. In that case, why assume that this something must be God? Why shouldn't it be the universe itself?

Supporters of the first-cause argument might respond that God is uniquely qualified to be the first cause, since he is the only logically necessary being. This answer is intriguing, but assumes the soundness of the ontological argument (see chapter 4).

A second objection to the first-cause argument concerns its assumption that the chain of causes that accounts for the existence of the universe can't extend backward forever. This assumption isn't necessarily correct. What's to say that the chain of causes *doesn't* extend back to infinity? While it's difficult to understand or imagine such a thing, the fact that we find something difficult to envisage doesn't necessarily mean that it's false. So perhaps the universe has always existed.

Once again, Aquinas foresaw this objection and had some respect for it. But he responded that even if the universe *has* existed forever, and even if the chain of causes *does* extend backward to infinity,

God is still necessary. Because even if we can account for every individual link in the chain of causation by assuming a prior cause, we still need to account for the existence of the entire chain.

criticisms of the design argument

According to the design argument, just as a watch bears evident marks of design and points to the existence of a watchmaker, so the universe bears evident marks of design and points to the existence of a wise and powerful creator. One objection to this argument is that the analogy between artifacts and natural objects is a weak one.

In his posthumously published *Dialogues Concerning Natural Religion*, the Scottish philosopher David Hume (see pages 172–5) pointed out that when we see a watch we are able to infer the existence of a watchmaker because we know by experience that this is how watches come about. But we can't make such inference with regard to the origin of the universe because we have no experience of how universes come about.

The contemporary British writer and philosopher Julian Baggini makes a related point in his book, *Atheism: A Very Short Introduction*. He says:

The analogy fails because the universe just isn't a mechanism like a watch. When we see a rabbit, for example, we do not look for a rabbit-maker. We think instead it had parents. Unlike artefacts, objects in the natural world emerge through natural processes, processes which are pretty well understood.

One such natural process is evolution. This widely accepted scientific theory provides an explanation of how complex organisms that are well adapted to their environments arise through random variation and natural selection rather than through design.

Another objection to the design argument is that even if we can infer the existence of a designer from the order and purpose we observe in nature, we can't infer the existence of an *all-knowing*, *all-powerful*, and *benevolent* creator. Only a perfect world could justify us in doing so, and the world we inhabit is far from perfect. Its creatures are not perfectly adapted to their environments. They become sick and grow old and die. They suffer pain and inflict pain upon one another. Some of them—including many humans— lead entirely wretched lives.

Given that the world contains so many imperfections and so many evils, it seems absurd to posit an all-knowing, all-powerful, all-loving creator. This brings us to the philosophy of religion's main argument for the nonexistence of God.

the problem of evil

The world contains suffering—and lots of it.

Some of this suffering arises from what philosophers term moral evil—that is, through human acts of cruelty, violence, greed, selfishness, and the like. And some of this suffering arises from what philosophers term natural evil—phenomena such as earthquakes, plagues, famine, and tsunamis.

Given that the world contains so much suffering, how can anyone take seriously the idea that it was created by an all-knowing, all-powerful, all-loving God? Such a being would surely have created a better world. This is the so-called "problem of evil," and it was expressed very neatly and concisely by Hume in his *Dialogues:*

> Is [God] willing to prevent evil, but not able? Then he is impotent. Is he able, but not willing? Then he is malevolent. Is he both able and willing? Whence then is evil?

responses to the problem of evil

Theists have offered a number of responses to the problem of evil, but they all have in common the idea that God allows moral and/or natural evils because this is somehow in our best interest.

For example, the free-will defense to the problem of evil states that God, rather than making us mere machines or automatons with no choice but to obey Him, has given us the inestimable gift of free will. A necessary consequence of this is that we are free to perform cruel and selfish acts if we wish to do so. By this account, God allows the possibility of moral evil because it is a price worth paying in the service of human autonomy.

Another response to the problem of evil seeks to account for the existence of natural evil by appealing to laws of nature. Laws of nature, so the argument goes, are essential to bring order and regularity to the world. Without them, the world would descend into chaos, and life would be impossible. On the whole, then, laws of nature act for our benefit. But sometimes the regular operation of these laws will bring about circumstances that may cause harm. God allows these natural evils because the alternative—a world of disorder—would be much worse.

the death of Bambi
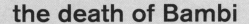

Theistic responses to the problem of evil, such as the free-will defense or the appeal to laws of nature, invariably claim that God allows certain kinds of suffering in order to serve some greater good.

The contemporary U.S. philosopher William Rowe, in his 1979 paper *The Problem of Evil and Some Varieties of Atheism*, countered such claims by pointing out that there exist in the world instances of intense suffering that serve no useful purpose and which an all-powerful, all-knowing, and benevolent God would prevent.

Rowe illustrates this by asking us to imagine a fawn which gets badly burned in a forest fire and which dies, days later, having suffered prolonged agony. Such suffering appears entirely pointless, so it seems reasonable to assume that a powerful and loving God would intervene.

And yet, every day creatures in the world suffer equally pointless suffering without divine intervention. So it seems reasonable to assume that an all-powerful, all-knowing, and benevolent God doesn't exist.

philosophy of mind

the mind/
body problem

The philosophy of mind is a major
branch of metaphysics. It investigates
the relationships between mental and
physical phenomena, especially that
between the mind and the body.

Important questions in the philosophy of
mind include, "What is a mind?", "How
do mind and body interact?", "Are mental
states reducible to physical ones?", and
"What can we know about other people's
mental states?"

The puzzle of the relationship between
the mind and the body is known as the
mind/body problem. It is the central issue
in the philosophy of mind and is the subject
that will occupy us throughout this chapter.

In his book *Confessions of a Philosopher*,
the philosophy writer Bryan Magee
describes how, as a child, he was puzzled
and intrigued by his ability to move a finger
by a mere act of thought. This is a specific
instance of a general sense of bewilderment
many of us feel when we stop to consider
the relationship between mental and bodily
processes. How can mental states, such as
thoughts, feelings, and ideas, affect what we
do with our bodies? And how can a physical
process, such as the firing of neurons in the
brain, give rise to conscious experience?

historical background

The nature of the mind/body relationship
has been debated since ancient times. The
Greek philosopher Parmenides (see page 74)
asserted that mental processes are ultimately
reducible to physical ones:

> **For it is the composition of body
> parts that does the thinking.**

Plato, on the other hand, emphasized the
radical difference between the mental
and the physical and held that the soul is
distinct from, and can exist independently
of, the body.

But it was Descartes who really opened
up the whole can of worms we now call the
mind/body problem. In his *Meditations on
First Philosophy*, he observed that the nature
of the mind (an immaterial nonextended,
thinking thing) and the nature of the body
(a material, extended, nonthinking thing)
are entirely different.

Furthermore, he noted that, although he
could doubt that he had a body, he couldn't
doubt that he had a mind. Therefore, since

the seat of the soul

Drawing on his extensive knowledge of 17th-century anatomy, Descartes suggested that the interaction between the mind and the body takes place in the pineal gland, a tiny organ deep in the center of the brain. He believed that the pineal gland is filled with animal spirits, "a certain very fine air or wind," which flow through the nerves, controlling the movements of the body and carrying sensory impressions to the soul. So the body is essentially a machine animated by a living soul, and the seat of the soul is the pineal gland.

However, Descartes was unable to explain how the immaterial mind could causally interact with the material body, and vice versa.

His idea seems to have been that the pineal gland was so very small, and the animal spirits were so very fine, that even the immaterial mind could move them. But, as his contemporaries were swift to point out, this was merely fudging the issue. The pineal gland and its contents, however small and light and fine, were nonetheless physical. So how could the nonphysical mind interact with them?

Despite this glaring weakness, Descartes's mind/body theory, known as Cartesian dualism, remained the dominant philosophical theory of the mind until the mid-20th century.

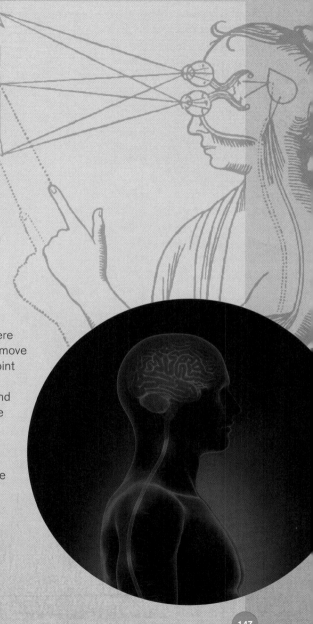

Leibniz's mill

In a short section of his 1714 work *Monadology*, the German philosopher Gottfried Leibniz illustrates the difficulty of explaining how conscious experience can arise from purely physical processes:

Supposing there were a machine, so constructed as to think, feel, and have perception, it might be conceived as increased in size, while keeping the same proportions, so that one might go into it as into a mill. That being so, we should, on examining its interior, find only parts which work one upon another, and never anything by which to explain a perception.

According to Leibniz, this demonstrates that thinking, sensing, and perceiving are not explicable on mechanical grounds and that mental phenomena are not reducible to physical processes.

The same kind of reasoning could be applied to the brain. However deeply we were to probe its workings, however fully we were to understand its chemical and electrical processes, we would never, it seems, find anything that resembles or explains consciousness.

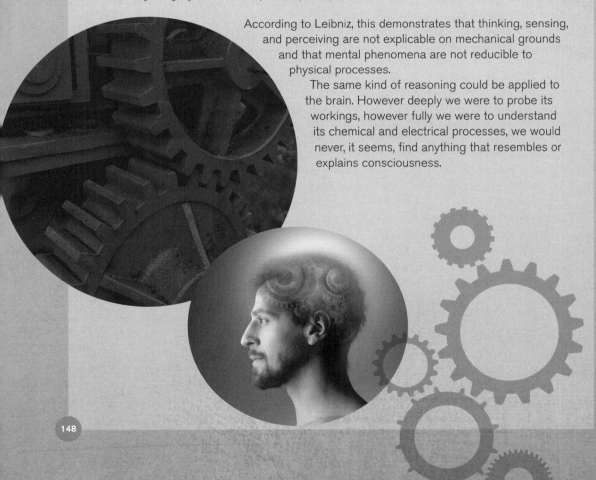

he *could* doubt the one thing but *couldn't* doubt the other, they must be two distinct things. These considerations led Descartes to conclude that each human consists of two parts: an immaterial substance, the mind, and a material substance, the body.

dualism

Mind/body dualism is the view that the body and the mind are two distinct things: a material and an immaterial substance respectively.

Mind/body dualists, such as Descartes, claim that the body is a material substance, whereas the mind is an immaterial substance, and that mental events are not reducible to physical processes.

One of the strongest motives for adopting dualism is the difficulty we have when we try to conceive how physical processes can possibly give rise to conscious experience.

the problem of interaction

To many people, the mental and physical realms appear so entirely different that dualism seems obviously correct. But despite its intuitive appeal, dualism has a serious flaw. It raises the troublesome question of how nonphysical minds and physical bodies can possibly interact.

That minds and bodies *do* interact seems beyond question. After all, by a simple act of will (a mental event) I can wiggle my toe (a physical event), and by injecting myself with an anesthetic (a physical event) I can dull myself to the experience of pain (a mental event). But if the mind and body are so very distinct, how can this be? How can mental events trigger physical events and vice versa?

This is known as the problem of interaction.

parallelism

The problem of interaction has proven so resistant to solution that some dualist philosophers have been driven to deny that mind/body interaction occurs at all. This seems bizarre. How can anyone deny what everyday experience seems so clearly to confirm?

Well, one theory, which is known as "parallelism" or "psychophysical parallelism," which was developed by Leibniz, states that mental and physical phenomena, rather than being causally linked, merely run in parallel.

To illustrate this theory, Leibniz likened the mind and the body to two clocks running independently from one another but in perfect synch. As a modern example, we could compare the clocks to two computers running independent but time-coordinated programs.

The mind is preset to register pain at the same time that the body touches something hot; the body is preset to move its legs at the same time that the mind forms the intention to walk; and so on. It appears that the mind and body are interacting, but they're not. They're just perfectly synchronized. There is, in Leibniz's phraseology, a "pre-established harmony" between them.

What did Leibniz think could possibly account for this incredibly sophisticated and accurate synchronization of all of the minds and bodies in the universe? Predictably, given his staunch theism, God.

occasionalism

Another, somewhat similar, attempt at sidestepping the problem of interaction is what is known as "occasionalism."

According to this theory, developed by the French philosopher and priest Nicolas Malebranche (1638–1715), mental events don't cause physical ones, and neither do physical events cause mental ones. There is, however, *something* that links the two kinds of events together. Once again, God.

According to Malebranche, when the body touches a flame, the mind feels pain. But the pain isn't caused by the flame. The pain is caused by God. The touching of the flame is merely the "occasion" which prompts God to cause the pain. Similarly, when the mind forms the intention to walk, the body moves its legs. But the mind's intention doesn't cause the legs to move. God does. The intention is merely the "occasion" that prompts God to move them.

Both parallelism and occasionalism invoke God's unlimited knowledge and power to circumvent the problem of mind/body interaction.

For Leibniz and Malebranche, this philosophical device seemed perfectly reasonable, since they both had independent reasons for believing in an omnipotent creator and sustainer of the universe.

But without those background beliefs, neither theory seems at all plausible. Indeed, modern philosophers tend to dismiss both parallelism and occasionalism as too fanciful to be taken seriously.

what's the difference?

Parallelism and occasionalism are similar responses to the problem of mind/body interaction. But there's a crucial difference. Parallelism sees God as having, in a sense, wound up the mental and physical worlds and then left them to follow their preset courses, whereas occasionalism sees God as being continuously and actively involved in making mental and physical events unfold in relation to one another.

physicalism

Despite its intuitive appeal, dualism raises a thorny problem. How can a nonphysical mind and a physical body conceivably interact? Many dualists have turned their attention to this problem, but as yet no plausible solution has been offered.

Given this fundamental weakness, many philosophers have now rejected dualism in favor of physicalism. According to physicalism, there is no immaterial mind, soul, or spirit. The mind is a physical thing, and every mental event is reducible to physical processes and properties.

Such diverse experiences as the pain that I get when I stub a toe, the colored image I perceive when I gaze upon a rainbow, and the nostalgic emotion I feel when thinking back to my childhood can all be accounted for in terms of what is happening to my body, especially my brain.

Physicalism has a tremendous advantage over dualism in that it dissolves the problem of interaction. Since it holds that the mind and body are both physical, there's no special difficulty accounting for their ability to causally affect one another.

Another strong point in physicalism's favor is that it accords well with our modern scientific approach to investigating and understanding the world. Modern science has had spectacular success in explaining and predicting a large variety of natural phenomena in terms of a small number of physical laws, and it has achieved this by focusing on what can be observed and measured. It seems reasonable, then, to take the view that the human mind might be explicable in the same terms and investigable by the same methods.

Physicalism holds that the mind, rather than being some mysterious and unfathomable immaterial entity, is just one more aspect of the material world and operates according to the same physical laws by which everything else does.

behaviorism

Of course, it's not enough for physicalists merely to assert that mental events can be accounted for in physical terms. They must also explain how this works. They must give an account of how physical processes in the body can produce thoughts, feelings, perceptions, and the like.

One theory, which was developed in the 1950s when physicalism first began to gain the ascendency over dualism, is known as behaviorism. In philosophy, behaviorism is the view that the mind, as such, doesn't exist, that descriptions of mental states are really just descriptions of people's actual or potential behavior.

By this account, to feel a pain is nothing more than to exhibit certain kinds of bodily reactions to negative stimuli and to be disposed to wince, moan, and cry out. Similarly, to believe that it is raining outside is nothing more than to have a tendency to put on waterproofs, carry an umbrella, or stay indoors.

According to the behaviorist, there's no mysterious nonphysical entity, "the mind." When we attribute a mind to someone, all we are really doing is attributing to them certain behavioral dispositions.

problems with behaviorism

The good thing about behaviorism is that it holds the promise of a thoroughly scientific understanding of what we call the mind. The bad thing about it is that it has some very serious flaws.

One common criticism of behaviorism is that it doesn't distinguish between such very different states as actually being in pain and merely pretending to be in pain, or actually being in love and merely pretending to be in love, and so on.

To this, the behaviorist might reasonably respond that some physical indications of pain or romantic love, such as changes in blood pressure or activation of the

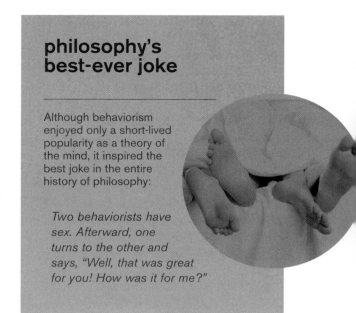

philosophy's best-ever joke

Although behaviorism enjoyed only a short-lived popularity as a theory of the mind, it inspired the best joke in the entire history of philosophy:

Two behaviorists have sex. Afterward, one turns to the other and says, "Well, that was great for you! How was it for me?"

dopamine system, can't be replicated by even the most skilled actor. So behaviorism does, in fact, distinguish between the actual and the pretended states.

Another objection involves causation. It seems an obvious fact that mental states sometimes cause behaviors. For example, the belief that a dog is vicious might cause someone to back away from it. But behaviorism cannot allow this. For the behaviorist, the belief that the dog is vicious *is* the backing away from it.

A third objection to behaviorism is that it takes no account of an essential aspect of mental experience—its conscious aspect, how it feels, what it's like. It may well be true that I learn about other people's mental states by observing their behavior. But that's not how I learn about my own mental states. I don't need to look in the mirror, or take my blood pressure, or monitor my behavior to know that I'm in pain, or in love, or seeing the color red. I simply consult my inner experience. Mental states such as these each have a subjective quality, or "qualia" (see page 157), about them, which behaviorism entirely fails to account for.

identity theory

Another proffered explanation of how physical processes can account for mental states is identity theory. This, which supplanted behaviorism in the mid-20th century, claims that every mental state is identical with some biological process in the brain. What this means, for example, is that for me to have a thought about, say, chicken nuggets, is just for my brain to be in a certain state, and for me to feel the pain of a toothache is just for my brain to be in a certain other state.

Identity theory claims that these mental events and the corresponding brain-states aren't merely related, they're *the same thing*. In the same way that a bolt of lightning *is* an electrical discharge, that ice *is* frozen water, and that a ray of light *is* an electromagnetic wave, a mental event *is* a brain-state.

According to identity theory, science will eventually discover which brain-states are identical with which mental states. This means that a neurologist of the future will be able to scrutinize a specific brain-state

and exclaim, "Ah, yes! This is a thought about the smell of freshly baked bread," or acknowledge, "This is a feeling of anxiety over a job interview."

problems with identity theory

Critics of identity theory point out that if thoughts, feelings, and suchlike are identical to brain-states, then they should have the same properties. But this doesn't appear to be the case.

One way in which they differ is that a conscious experience is a private and subjective thing, whereas a brain-state is a publicly observable and objective thing. If a neurologist were to examine your brain-state (the various neurons, impulses, chemical reactions) she would be seeing something that *anyone* could observe. But the associated conscious experience is something that *only you* can observe.

Furthermore, a thought is always *about* something. For example, a thought might be about a lump of cheese or the Great Wall of China. But a brain-state is isn't about anything. It doesn't relate to anything outside itself.

These examples suggest that conscious experiences and brain-states have different properties. So doesn't that imply they're different things?

Another objection to identity theory again concerns "qualia," discussed on page 157. Like behaviorism, identity theory can't account for the subjective quality of mental events—for the way they feel.

No description of a brain-state, however detailed and accurate, could ever capture what a pain, or a visual sensation, or a desire is actually *like*.

functionalism

A currently popular materialist theory of mind is functionalism. The philosophers who developed this took their inspiration from the world of computing.

Essentially, what a computer does is receive some kind of input, process it, and then produce some kind of related output. Functionalism views the body and mind in a similar way. The brain is like the computer or hardware, and the mind is like the computer program or software.

Functionalism focuses on the functional role of mental states. It defines mental states in terms of the relationships between perceptual inputs and behavioral outputs.

So, for example, to say that someone experiences fear when confronted by a large dog is to say that there is some kind of process going on inside them that connects a certain set of inputs (seeing the dog, hearing the dog, etc.) to a certain set of outputs (increased respiration, shaking limbs, backing away, etc.).

Unlike behaviorism, functionalism allows that mental states can play a causal role in determining other mental events and in determining behavior.

So, someone's belief that a dog is vicious rather than friendly can cause them to experience fear when they encounter the dog, and, consequently, this can influence their behavior. Beliefs, intentions, desires, and the like are—to return to the computer analogy—part of the active software of the mind.

For the functionalist, the mind is to be understood in terms of its function. That is, in terms of what it does rather than the stuff it's made from.

functionalism and dualism

Although functionalism is generally considered a materialist theory of mind, it is, strictly speaking, compatible with dualism, too.

Functionalism holds that the mind is to be understood in terms of its function. So anything that can process sensory inputs and behavioral outputs in the appropriate manner can be considered a mind. This could be a human brain, an android's circuitry, the noncarbon-based central nervous system of an alien or—as the dualists contend—a Cartesian immaterial substance.

This means that anything with the ability to link sensory inputs to behavioral outputs in the way that a human does (a robot, for example) could be said to have a mind.

Furthermore, any two things that were to link inputs and outputs together in precisely the same way could be said to have identical minds and identical mental states.

problems with functionalism

Like other materialist theories of the mind, functionalism is frequently criticized for failing to account for the conscious aspects of mental experience.

the problem of consciousness

Although mind/body dualism has a lot of intuitive appeal, it has been rejected by many modern philosophers in favor of materialism. This is, in large part, down to the inability of dualists to offer a satisfactory solution to the problem of interaction (see page 149).

Materialism, like dualism, has its problems. Chief among these is the difficulty of accounting for the subjective aspects of mental experience. This is known as the problem of consciousness. This problem is so pronounced that it has led some philosophers to question whether materialism is, after all, a superior philosophy of mind to dualism.

Consider the case of two people who experience colors differently. Perhaps one of them sees red and green the same way that you and I do, but the other sees red the way that you and I see green, and vice versa.

Both of them are capable of recognizing red objects and can distinguish red from other colors, but each of them has a different inner experience. Red looks and feels a different way to each of them.

Now imagine they are shown a red apple. Both report that it looks red. They have an identical behavioral response to the same sensory input. So, according to functionalism their mental states are, in this respect, identical.

But, critics argue, this means that functionalism is false, because their mental states *are not* identical. Their subjective experience of seeing the color red is entirely different.

the ghost in the machine

Most people are familiar with the phrase "the ghost in the machine." It was first used by the British philosopher Gilbert Ryle (1900–76) in his 1949 book *The Concept of Mind*.

Ryle was an early champion of materialism and advocate of behaviorism, and he used the phrase to deride the doctrine—or rather, as he termed it, the "dogma"—of mind/body dualism.

qualia

Philosophers use the term "qualia" to label the subjective qualities of conscious experience.

The U.S. philosopher Daniel Dennett, defines qualia as: "an unfamiliar term for something that could not be more familiar to each of us: the ways things seem to us."

Seeing red, tasting wine, and hearing a clap of thunder—all of these experiences feel to us a certain way. There is a certain *what-it's-like* quality to each one. This is what philosophers mean by qualia.

It's not only perceptions and sensations that have qualia. So, too, do emotions, moods, and perhaps even thoughts.

No physical description, however full, can ever capture the qualia of conscious experience. Nothing you could say to an unsighted person could convey the experience of actually *seeing* red, and no amount of neurological and physiological data could convey the itchiness of an itch.

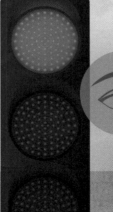

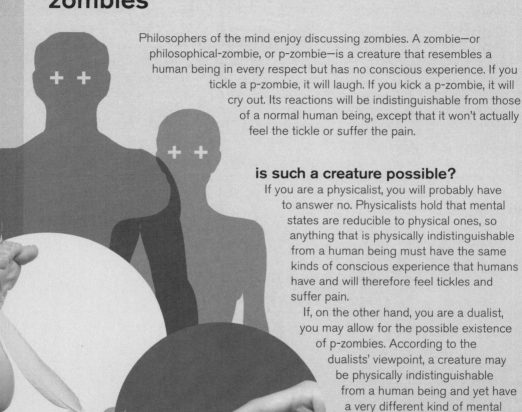

zombies

Philosophers of the mind enjoy discussing zombies. A zombie—or philosophical-zombie, or p-zombie—is a creature that resembles a human being in every respect but has no conscious experience. If you tickle a p-zombie, it will laugh. If you kick a p-zombie, it will cry out. Its reactions will be indistinguishable from those of a normal human being, except that it won't actually feel the tickle or suffer the pain.

is such a creature possible?

If you are a physicalist, you will probably have to answer no. Physicalists hold that mental states are reducible to physical ones, so anything that is physically indistinguishable from a human being must have the same kinds of conscious experience that humans have and will therefore feel tickles and suffer pain.

If, on the other hand, you are a dualist, you may allow for the possible existence of p-zombies. According to the dualists' viewpoint, a creature may be physically indistinguishable from a human being and yet have a very different kind of mental experience—or even no mental experience at all. In fact, the most famous dualist of all, Descartes, believed that animals are mere automatons: complex machines lacking any mental life—animal versions of p-zombies, if you like.

Mary's room

In the 1980s, the contemporary Australian philosopher Frank Jackson put forward a strong argument against physicalism, which he presented in the form a thought-experiment, known as Mary's Room.

Mary—so the story goes—has lived her entire life in a controlled environment where her visual experiences have been limited to seeing black, white, and shades of gray. She is, nevertheless, a talented scientist and an expert on the neurophysiology of vision. She knows which wavelengths of light stimulate which nerves in the retina. She understands the process by which these nerves transmit impulses to the brain. She has a thorough knowledge of the electrochemical changes that take place in the brain as a result. And she knows how these brain-states translate to people's reported experiences of, and behavioral responses to, seeing colors. In fact, for the purposes of this thought-experiment, it is assumed that Mary knows everything there is physically to know about color perception.

Then, one day, Mary is presented with a ripe tomato. Will she learn anything new? Yes, she will learn what it's like actually to *see* red. This shows that her previous knowledge was incomplete. Although she knew everything there was physically to know about seeing colors, there was, nonetheless, something she *didn't* know. This means that there must be something more to seeing than the purely physical.

In his 1982 essay *Epiphenomenal Qualia* Jackson writes:

Tell me everything physical there is to tell about what is going on in a living brain, the kind of states, their functional role, their relation to what goes on at other times and in other brains, and so on and so forth, and be I as clever as can be in fitting it all together, you won't have told me about the hurtfulness of pains, the itchiness of itches, pangs of jealousy, or about the characteristic experience of tasting a lemon, smelling a rose, hearing a loud noise or seeing the sky.

Jackson's argument, in a nutshell, is that knowledge of all relevant physical facts tells you nothing about the qualitative aspects of conscious experience, but physicalism maintains that the physical facts are all of the facts, so physicalism must be false. This is known as the "knowledge argument."

those powers. But now we know better, and science provides a superior explanation for such events in physical terms. Demons and witches are no longer part of our ontological or explanatory framework.

eliminative materialism

Eliminative materialists claim that, in the same way, the time will come when our folk beliefs in desires, fears, sensations, pains, and joys will also be put aside in favor of neuroscientific descriptions.

As the American philosopher and writer Edward Feser humorously remarks in his discussion of eliminative materialism in *Philosophy of Mind: A Beginner's Guide*:

> Perhaps the citizens of eliminative materialist societies of the future will no longer say things like, "Boy! This pain is really getting to me," but rather "there's a particularly high level of activity in my C-fibers and reticular formation."

property dualism

Some philosophers have responded to the problems inherent in both dualism and materialism in a more subtle way by advocating a new form of dualism, a kind of hybrid of dualism and materialism, known as property dualism.

Traditional dualism—which can now be labeled substance dualism—is the view, associated with Descartes, that the world contains two kinds of substance, physical and mental. Property dualism doesn't

the new dualism

Just as the problem of interaction is a thorn in the side of dualism, the problem of consciousness is a perennial problem for materialism.

Some philosophers, acutely aware of the problem of consciousness but still convinced of the truth of materialism, have responded in a startling—and rather bizarre—manner by denying that consciousness exists. They adopt the position, known as eliminative materialism, that our common-sense view of the mind is wrong, that we don't have minds, and neither do we have thoughts, feelings, ideas, or experiences. Talk of such things is mere folk psychology, an unscientific way of trying to account for psychological phenomena.

People used to believe in the supernatural powers of demons and witches and accounted for certain events in terms of claim that the world contains two kinds of substance but rather two kinds of property.

By this account, your brain is composed of only one kind of stuff, but that stuff has two entirely different sets of properties, physical and mental. Its physical properties include its shape, size, mass, color, and every other property that can be described by physics. Its mental properties include consciousness, thoughts, feelings, intentions, and suchlike.

Mental properties can't be reduced to physical properties, and vice versa. This means that thoughts and feelings can't be translated into physical properties such as brain-states, however full and accurate those descriptions might be.

epiphenomenalism

One theory that offers such a compromise between dualism and materialism is epiphenomenalism. According to this, physical events can produce mental events, but not the other way around. Mental events exert no causal influence upon the brain or the rest of the body. Mental events exist—they are by-products of complex physical processes, but they're inert. They don't cause physical events and neither do they cause other mental events.

Mental phenomena—thoughts, feelings, awareness, for example—can be likened to the steam whistle on a locomotive. The machinery of the locomotive produces the whistle, but the whistle contributes nothing to the workings of the locomotive. Similarly, mental phenomena are produced by brain processes, but mental phenomena themselves produce nothing. The mind is an epiphenomenon, a secondary phenomenon that results from and accompanies another.

At first, epiphenomenalism sounds quite plausible, but further reflection shows it to be counterintuitive. It implies that when I feel a sudden pain, the pain doesn't make me flinch, and when I decide to kick a ball, the intention doesn't cause the kick. The flinching and the kicking are caused by wholly unconscious brain activities, and the pain and the intention are just by-products of these processes.

Spinoza: extension and mind

Substance dualism is associated with the American philosopher Donald Davidson, who introduced it in his 1970 essay *Mental Events*.

But its roots can be traced back to the 17th-century Dutch philosopher Baruch Spinoza, who held that existence has two aspects: extension (occupying physical space) and mind.

In his *Ethics* (first published in 1677), Spinoza wrote:

Mind and body are one and the same individual, conceived now under the attribute of thought, now under the attribute of extension.

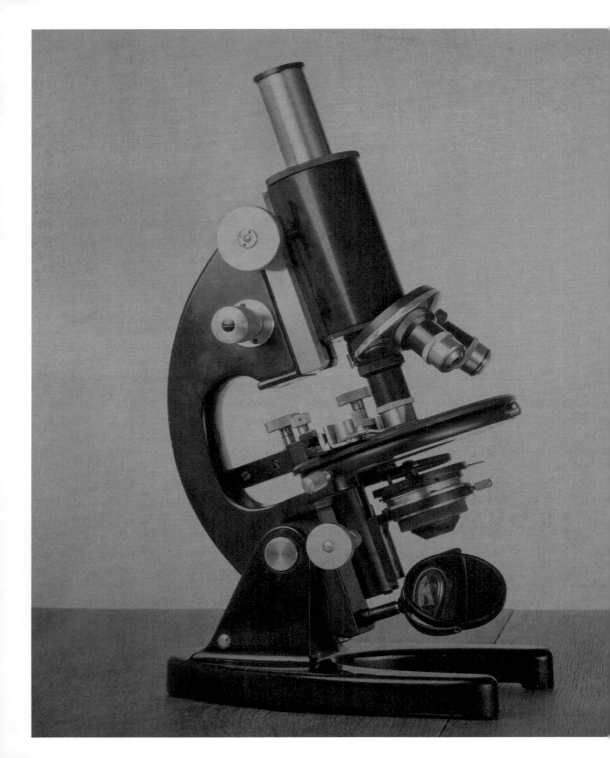

philosophy
of science

what is science?

Philosophy of science is a branch of philosophy that investigates science and scientific method. It seeks the answers to two types of question: 1) epistemological questions concerning the justification and reliability of science; and 2) metaphysical questions concerning the nature of the reality that science reveals.

Some of the big questions in the philosophy of science are, "What is science?", "What distinguishes science from non-science?", "How reliable is science?", and "What is the relationship between science and truth?"

special status

Science enjoys a special status in modern society. It's generally acknowledged to be our best and

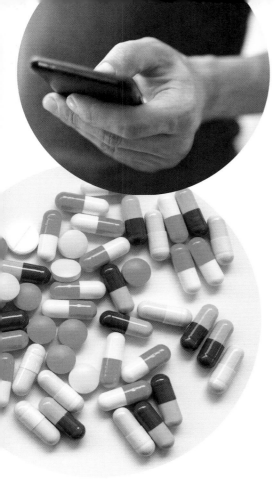

sometimes used in ways that are harmful to us and to the planet. But there's no denying that—whether used for good or ill—science works.

the art of science

Science owes its spectacular success to its methodology, its uniquely powerful procedures for acquiring, interpreting, and utilizing facts about the physical world. But what is this method? How does science work?

There is no straightforward answer to this, and it's one of the questions that philosophers of science spend their time pondering. But we'll begin this chapter by describing a widely held common-sense view of scientific method, which many scientists would endorse.

The *Oxford Dictionary* defines scientific method as: "a method of procedure that has characterized natural science since the 17th century, consisting in systematic observation, measurement, and experiment, and the formulation, testing, and modification of hypotheses."

It's a good, concise definition—but rather *too* concise for our purposes. So let's unpackage it.

the center of the universe

The birth of modern science may, as the dictionary suggests, have taken place in the 17th century, but the act of conception took place a little earlier, in 1542. This was the year in which the Polish astronomer

most reliable source of knowledge about the world and how it works. Science allows us to predict a huge variety of physical events with stunning accuracy. It enables us to control our environment in ways that would have amazed and terrified our ancestors. It has given us airplanes, computers, antibiotics, TVs, microwave ovens, space telescopes, cellphones, artificial hearts… Needless to say, scientific knowledge is

Nicolaus Copernicus (1473–1543) published *De revolutionibus orbium coelestium* (*On the Revolutions of the Heavenly Spheres*).

Copernicus's revolutionary work put the sun at the center of the universe, and placed the earth and the rest of the planets in orbit around it. This *heliocentric* (sun-centered) theory of the cosmos challenged the then-dominant *geocentric* (earth-centered) theory, and in so doing cast doubt upon the intellectual authority of Aristotle and the Bible (see chapter 1).

Despite initial opposition from the Church (*De revolutionibus* was placed on the Index of Forbidden Books) Copernicus's ideas inspired a number of subsequent thinkers, including the German astronomer and mathematician Johannes Kepler (1571–1630) and the Italian physicist, astronomer, and mathematician Galileo Galilei (1564–1642). Galileo was foremost among a new breed of natural philosophers who, in the 17th century, ushered in the era of modern science by insisting that theories about the world be based firmly and entirely upon observable facts.

formulation and modification of hypotheses

Science isn't only about gathering facts to test theories; it's also about formulating new and better theories. It's a creative process.

Scientists don't simply amass data, they look for patterns in that data and attempt to construct theories to account for those patterns. They seek to explain the facts in terms of general laws.

A paradigm example is Newton's Universal Law of Gravitation. Isaac Newton (1642–1727) was an English physicist and mathematician and arguably the most influential scientist of all time. One of his greatest achievements was his formulation of the law of gravitation, which states

observation, measurement, and experiment

Galileo is generally regarded as the first modern physicist. One reason for this is that he was the first natural philosopher to show that physical events could be described in mathematical terms. Another was his insistence upon the systematic testing of hypotheses (see page 168).

For Galileo, it wasn't enough that a theory seemed plausible or that it was compatible with the pronouncements of authorities such as Aristotle and the Church. It had to be put to the test. It had to conform to the facts. And it had to be confirmed by observation, measurement, and experiment.

This stubborn insistence upon rigorous and wide-ranging testing was innovative in Galileo's day but has been a fundamental feature of scientific investigation ever since.

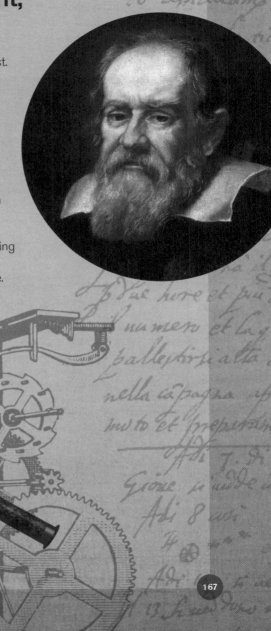

falling bodies and mountains on the moon

According to Aristotelian physics, heavier bodies will fall faster than lighter ones. Common sense concurs. After all, if you drop a feather and a stone simultaneously, the stone will plummet to earth while the feather will drift gently downward.

Galileo wasn't convinced. He believed that the stone and feather only fall at different rates because of air-resistance effects. In a vacuum, he claimed, they would fall at precisely the same rate. Legend has it that Galileo tested and confirmed his theory by dropping balls of different weights from the Leaning Tower of Pisa. The tale is apocryphal, but what certainly is true is that Galileo conducted extensive tests of his theory by rolling balls of different weights down inclined planes to slow them down enough to measure their motion. These experiments provided strong supporting evidence for his theory, which was later conclusively proved.

Aristotle had also claimed that the Earth is the center of the Cosmos, and that the Sun, Moon, stars, and planets, which are all perfect, unchanging spheres, revolve around it.

But when Galileo investigated the skies, with a telescope of his own design, he observed sun-spots, the moons of Jupiter, the "handles" of Saturn, mountains and craters on the Moon, and the phases of Venus.

All of these observations conflicted with Aristotle's cosmology, and were instrumental in converting the scientific community to Copernicus's heliocentric model of the Cosmos.

that any two bodies in the universe attract each other with a force that is directly proportional to the product of their masses and inversely proportional to the square of the distance between them.

This simple, precise, and concise law, in combination with Newton's earlier three laws of motion, was able to explain and to predict a wide range of natural phenomena, including planetary motion, projectile motion, and tidal effects. Formulating it required not only an immense knowledge and understanding of science and mathematics but also imaginative and creative genius.

Newton's theories possessed such extraordinary explanatory and predictive power that for more than 200 years it seemed that they were capable—in principle, at least—of explaining everything.

Nonetheless, in science, even the best-attested and most long-standing theories must be continually reassessed in the light of new facts. And, in the early 20th century, Newton's laws were shown to give incorrect results when applied to very massive objects, to very fast-moving objects, and to subatomic particles. These new findings gave rise to relativity theory and quantum mechanics.

in a nutshell

Science, then, owes its unique success to the method established by natural philosophers, such as Galileo and Newton, in the 17th century. It consists

natural philosophy

The term "natural philosophy" refers to the philosophical study of nature, as it was practiced prior to the scientific revolution of the 17th century. However, the English word "scientist" wasn't coined until the 19th century, so early scientists such as Galileo and Newton continued to think of and describe themselves as natural philosophers.

of observation and experiment, the formulation of hypotheses, and the testing and modification of hypotheses.

observation & theory

The most significant and distinctive feature of science is that it is derived from facts. Science isn't about opinion or speculation; its theories are based upon cold, hard facts that are determined by reliable and impartial observations. Many scientists would endorse this widely held view of science—but it isn't entirely true.

When two people observe the same object, they don't necessarily have the same visual experience, not even if they view it under identical conditions and not even if they have identical images on their retinas.

To be convinced that this is the case, take a look at the diagram here. It's likely that you'll see a staircase with the upper side of the stairs showing. But, if you continue

to look, you'll find that after a while your perception will change. What you will see is a staircase showing the underside of the staircase. With practice, you'll be able to switch between these alternative perceptions at will. But that's not all. When members of certain African tribes, who were unfamiliar with perspectival drawings, were shown the same diagram, they didn't see a staircase at all, just a two-dimensional pattern.

So the identical image can be perceived in very different ways by different observers, and the way it is perceived depends very much upon the individual observer's expectations and experiences.

observations are theory-laden

There's more to seeing, then, than meets the eye. What we expect to see can sometimes affect what we do see. Some philosophers believe that this casts doubt on the view that scientific observations are objective and unbiased.

The American philosopher of science N. R. Hanson (1924–67), for example, claimed that all observations are theory-laden—in other words, that scientists' theoretical presuppositions affect their observations. A doctor studying an X-ray sees something quite different from what a layperson sees looking at the same X-ray.

The same goes for a physicist studying an image produced by an electron microscope. In all cases, what the expert sees is partly determined by his or her beliefs.

A telling example of this concerns positrons. The existence of these antimatter particles was first predicted by the British physicist Paul Dirac (1902–84) in 1928. Prior to this, scientists routinely failed to notice their tracks in cloud chambers. Modern particle physicists looking back on the same experimental data see their tracks quite clearly.

observation statements are theory-laden

The statements that scientists use to report their observations are theory-laden, too.

For example, a scientist might report that in a certain experiment the strength of the magnetic field surrounding a coil of wire increased, but this statement is loaded with theoretical assumptions regarding the nature of magnetic fields and the methods used to detect them. Strictly speaking, the scientist doesn't observe the strength of the magnetic field at all. It is inferred from the readings on the instruments.

Does it matter?

Some philosophers of science have argued that theory-ladenness matters a great deal. If all observations are theory-laden, they say, then observations can't be used to make neutral comparisons between competing theories. Others disagree. They say that there are plenty of commonly accepted background beliefs that scientists can appeal to when comparing one theory with another.

Paul is dead!

It's not only visual experiences that are affected by our expectations and experiences.

When I discovered the Beatles as a teenager, I was fascinated by the "Paul is dead" conspiracy theory, according to which Paul McCartney died in a car crash in 1966 and was replaced by a lookalike.

The theory was supported by various items of "evidence," mostly in the form of "clues" hidden in Beatles songs and album artwork. One such clue is found in the instrumental section at the end of the song "Strawberry Fields Forever," in which, it is said, if you listen carefully, you can hear John Lennon growling, "I buried Paul."

When I first heard about this, I played the song and discovered that you can indeed hear those words. Later, I read that John Lennon claimed his actual words were "cranberry sauce." I played the song and discovered that he was telling the truth.

In both cases, I heard precisely what I expected to hear.

David Hume

The Scottish philosopher David Hume (1711–76) is one of the most important figures in Western philosophy. In the fields of epistemology, metaphysics, and ethics his ideas and arguments have been enormously influential.

Hume was a staunch empiricist and a radical skeptic who considered his predecessors to have vastly overestimated the powers of human reason and the possible extent of human knowledge. His claim that causal inferences cannot be rationally justified and his classic statement of the problem of induction are fundamental to the philosophy of science.

Hume's life and works

At age 12, Hume entered the University of Edinburgh, where he studied law. After a few years, he left the university to devote himself to private study and to philosophy. In 1734 he wrote *A Treatise of Human Nature*. This comprehensive work was pretty much ignored at the time but eventually came to be recognized as one of the most significant contributions to philosophy. Hume's intention in writing the *Treatise* was to develop a "science of man." He wanted to apply Newton's "experimental method of reasoning" to the study of human nature in order to discover the principles governing human thoughts, behavior, and emotions. His conclusions were profoundly skeptical. He claimed that most of our behavior is governed by passion and instinct rather than reason.

In his lifetime, he was best known as a historian and man of letters. His six-volume *History of England* (1754–61) won him great wealth, fame, and acclaim. His *Dialogues Concerning Natural Religion*, begun in 1750, was published posthumously in 1779. It is a seminal work in the philosophy of religion, in which three philosophers—Demea, Philo, and Cleanthes—discuss the existence and nature of God. It has some of the strongest arguments ever advanced in support of religious skepticism and agnosticism.

relations of ideas and matters of fact

According to Hume, there are just two valid objects of human inquiry: relations of ideas and matters of fact.

Relations of ideas include, "the sciences of geometry, algebra, and arithmetic, and in short, every affirmation which is either intuitively or demonstratively certain."

Hume's fork

The principle that human knowledge is restricted to relations of ideas and matters of fact may appear to be innocuous, but Hume uses it to wreak philosophical havoc.

Whenever we are presented with some claim to knowledge, he says, we must inquire into its source. Is it derived from some demonstrably certain relation of ideas, or is it a matter of empirical fact, confirmed by experience?

If the answer is neither, then it isn't knowledge. It is mere speculation.

This doctrine is often referred to as Hume's fork. Hume used it to dismiss many of the metaphysical claims of the rationalists— for example, claims about the existence and nature of God, the soul, and absolute moral values. Such knowledge, Hume argues, isn't derived from demonstrable relationships between clear and unambiguous ideas. Neither is it derived from sensory investigation of the world. Therefore, it isn't knowledge at all.

In a famous and stirring passage from his 1748 work, *An Enquiry Concerning Human Understanding*, he writes:

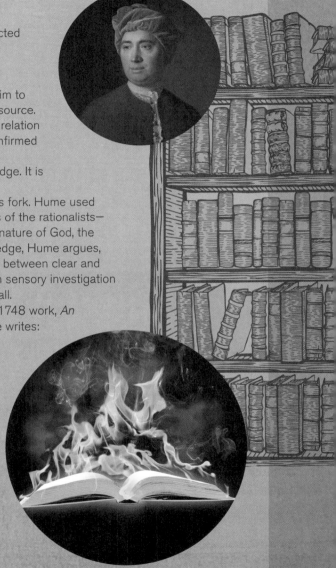

> *When we run over libraries, persuaded of these principles, what havoc must we make? If we take in our hand any volume; of divinity or school metaphysics, for instance; let us ask, Does it contain any abstract reasoning concerning quantity or number? No. Does it contain any experimental reasoning concerning matter of fact and existence? No. Commit it then to the flames: For it can contain nothing but sophistry and illusion.*

173

These express nothing more than the relationships between various concepts and are discoverable by the mere operation of thought. They are demonstrably true and cannot be denied without contradiction.

Matters of fact, on the other hand, "are not ascertained in the same manner; nor is our evidence of their truth, however great, of a like nature with [relations of ideas]." These are statements about the world, and such knowledge can't be acquired through the mere operation of thought but only through empirical investigation (see page 80). The contrary to every matter of fact is perfectly conceivable and involves no contradiction. For example, the proposition "copper doesn't conduct electricity," although factually incorrect, is a thoroughly intelligible proposition. It can be proven wrong only by testing and not by an appeal to logic.

the problem of induction

Imagine that you were to shoot one billiard ball into another. What would happen? Clearly, the first ball would set the second in motion. We all know that. But how do we know? David Hume asked himself this question and came up with a startling answer—we don't.

cause and effect

Hume claimed that every item of human knowledge is either derived logically from relations of ideas or established empirically as a matter of fact.

So, what about our knowledge of billiard-ball collisions?

Hume says that this isn't—and couldn't be—derived from relations of ideas. When we contemplate one ball striking another, we can conceive of any number of outcomes. The first ball might stop dead when it meets the second, or it might rebound, or it might jump up into the air. Similarly, the second ball might remain motionless, or it might shoot off in any direction, or it might explode. No amount of *a priori* reasoning can connect the antecedents of this event with the consequences, the cause with the effect.

So is our knowledge, in this case, established empirically as a matter of fact?

Yes, says Hume. We know what happens when one ball collides with another because we have witnessed many such events before.

The same applies to causation in general. We can never discover any logical relationship between causes and their effects. We only observe that certain effects have invariably followed from certain causes. Hume writes:

> I shall venture to affirm, as a general proposition, which admits of no exception, that the knowledge of [cause and effect] is not, in any instance, attained by reasonings a priori; but arises entirely from experience, when we find that any particular objects are constantly conjoined with each other. Let an object be presented to a man of ever so strong natural reason and abilities; if that object be entirely new to him, he will not be able, by the most accurate examination of its sensible qualities, to discover any of its causes or effects.

the problem of induction

Strictly speaking, our knowledge of such matters is limited to those cases that we have actually observed.

We know that on previous occasions when one billiard ball has struck another, the second ball has moved, but we don't know that this is what always happens nor can we know that it will continue to happen in the future. This is because our entire knowledge of causes and effects is based upon induction, a method of reasoning whereby we draw general conclusions from a limited number of observations. It relies upon the assumptions that, in Hume's words, "instances of which we have had no experience, must resemble those of which we have had experience, and that the course of nature continues always uniformly the same."

But what justifies these assumptions?

Hume claims that nothing does, that we can't provide any rational justification of induction. The claim that nature is, and will remain, uniform isn't a logical truth. There's no logical contradiction involved in supposing that the way the universe operates in the future might be different from the way it has operated in the past.

The claim that nature will continue to operate in the future as it has in the past isn't something we can know from experience either, because all our experience is of the past, and the very point at issue is whether regularities that have held in the past will continue to do so in the future.

Hume claims, then, that inductive reasoning can't be rationally justified. We use it and rely upon it all the time—it has served us well in the past—but we have no grounds for thinking that it will continue to serve us well in the future.

induction in science

The problem of induction is a major headache for philosophers of science.

Science is, after all, reliant upon induction. It relies upon using a limited number of observations to formulate general laws and predict future events. So, if induction can't be rationally justified, neither, it seems, can science.

falsification

According to falsificationism, science isn't so much about trying to confirm theories as trying to refute them.

Taking the common-sense view of science, which we examined in the first section of this chapter, scientific method proceeds along the following lines. First, the scientist makes a number of impartial observations. Then she constructs a theory to explain those observations. Then she tests her theory and modifies it as required. Eventually, if it survives prolonged and rigorous testing, the theory is confirmed as valid, or correct.

confirmation impossible

We have already seen that there is a problem with this simple view of science, namely, that observations are seldom, if ever, impartial. Another difficulty—and a bigger one—concerns confirmation. No scientific theory can ever be conclusively verified. No matter how much evidence we amass in its support and no matter how many tests it survives, we can never be entirely sure that it is correct.

This is because scientific theories and laws are confirmed by induction. And, as we learned in chapter 2 (see pages 37–38), inductive arguments never guarantee the truth of their conclusions. They never lead to certainty.

We can illustrate this with an example.

Einstein's special theory of relativity, which he published in 1905, predicted, among other things, that nothing can travel faster than the speed of light. This prediction has been subjected to the most wide-ranging and rigorous testing for more than a century and has survived every test.

So, in order to confirm the truth of Einstein's nothing-travels-faster-than-light principle, we could offer the following inductive argument:

**Nothing has ever been observed to travel faster than the speed of light.
Therefore nothing travels faster than the speed of light.**

But the truth of the premise doesn't logically guarantee the truth of the conclusion. There's always the possibility that at some future date something might be observed to move faster than the speed of light.

Despite a vast amount of entirely confirmatory evidence, Einstein's speed-of-light principle hasn't been—and never could be—conclusively verified.

Hume revisited

In fact, the problem regarding induction and its role in confirmation runs even deeper than the previous example suggests.

As we learned, Hume argued that the use of induction can't be rationally justified at all and that we have no reason to assume that the universe will continue to operate in the future as it has in the past. If Hume is correct, then science seems to be built upon a very shaky foundation.

Popper and falsification

The Austrian-born British philosopher Karl Popper (1902–94) was acutely aware of the problem of induction and the doubt it casts upon the validity of scientific theories.

He agreed that, because of the problem of induction, scientific theories can never be confirmed, but he claimed that this doesn't matter, because, despite appearances, science isn't really about confirmation; it isn't about proving theories right. It's about falsification—proving theories wrong.

Although scientific theories can never be confirmed, they can be falsified. This is because there's an asymmetry between verification and falsification. Even though no amount of evidence can confirm a theory, a single piece of reliable evidence can falsify one. Confirmation fails because it relies upon induction. Falsification succeeds because it is based upon deduction.

The following argument is a deductive one. So if the premise is true, the conclusion is guaranteed to be true as well.

Something was reliably observed to travel faster than the speed of light.
Therefore the theory that nothing travels faster than the speed of light is false.

falsificationism

According to Popper, science proceeds along the following lines.

The scientist starts with a problem, with some aspect of the world that needs explaining. Then she formulates a theory that offers a solution to that problem. Then she subjects her theory to rigorous testing in an attempt to refute it. If the theory survives testing it is provisionally accepted. It isn't confirmed—that's not possible—but it is "corroborated." Since science progresses by a process of falsification, says Popper, all proper scientific theories must be capable of being falsified. Furthermore, the more falsifiable they are, the better they are. The best scientific theories make bold claims. They make risky predictions that can be tested and, if false, shown to be false.

For example, Einstein's general theory of relativity, which he published in 1915, predicted that starlight passing close to the sun would have its path bent by the sun's gravitational field.

In 1919, a total solar eclipse provided suitable conditions to test this prediction. Starlight was bent, just as Einstein predicted it would be, and his theory was corroborated. But there was always the possibility that his prediction would fail, in which case his theory would have been falsified. No ifs, no buts, and no excuses.

criticisms of falsification

One common criticism of falsificationism is that it doesn't do justice to the role of confirmation in science; it fails to account for the fact that theories *do* get a boost when they make successful predictions. As we saw previously, Einstein's general theory of relativity received a huge boost when its prediction about the bending of starlight was confirmed during the solar eclipse of 1919.

This is not a real problem for falsification. In fact, Popper entirely agreed that scientific theories receive strong corroboration when they make bold predictions that are subsequently borne out by observation. But the point is that strong corroboration only occurs with highly falsifiable predictions. Furthermore, the principle still holds that one reliable falsifying observation is of more logical account than any number of confirmatory ones.

Another criticism of falsificationism is that its account of scientific progress is at odds with the facts. The history of science contains lots of examples of theories that were retained despite being falsified, or apparently falsified, by the available evidence.

To take just one example, the orbit of the planet Mercury was known for many years to differ from that predicted by Newtonian mechanics. Yet this didn't lead to the rejection of Newton's theories—at least not until Einstein's general theory of relativity came along and predicted the correct orbit.

Examples such as this one show that scientists are not always so ready to discard falsified theories as falsificationism claims they should.

science and pseudoscience

Karl Popper's interest in the philosophy of science began with his attempt to understand what it is that sets science apart from non-science.

He was deeply impressed by theories of physics, such as Einstein's theories of relativity, but unimpressed by certain theories in psychology and sociology, such as psychoanalysis and Marxism.

Followers of Freud and Marx often claimed that their respective founders' theories were scientific, but Popper wasn't convinced. Although initially attracted to both psychoanalysis and Marxism, he soon grew disillusioned with them. He felt that these theories, "though posing as science, had in fact more in common with primitive myths than with science; that they resembled astrology rather than astronomy."

He eventually decided that the problem with them—the thing that makes them unscientific— is that they do not make testable, falsifiable predictions. Their followers are too eager to collect evidence that confirms their beliefs, and too reluctant to seek out and to countenance evidence that falsifies them.

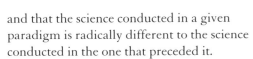

scientific revolutions

Thomas Kuhn (1922–96) was an American historian of science. His 1962 book *The Structure of Scientific Revolutions* sparked a revolution in the philosophy of science by claiming that scientific progress involves "paradigm shifts": radically different ways of viewing the world and conducting research.

Kuhn started out as a physicist before turning his attention to the history and philosophy of science. His understanding of the history of science led him to reject the traditional view that science progresses smoothly via the gradual acquisition of knowledge and the continual reappraisal of theories in the light of new evidence. Instead he claimed that scientific progress involves leaps from one conceptual framework—or "paradigm"— to another, and that the science conducted in a given paradigm is radically different to the science conducted in the one that preceded it.

An example of a paradigm shift is that from the Aristotelian world-view to the Newtonian one. As we saw on pages 165–69, this involved not only the adoption of a new cosmology, but also a whole new approach to experimentation and the interpretation of evidence. Another example of a paradigm shift is that which took place in the first half of the 20th century from Newtonian mechanics to quantum theory and general relativity.

normal and revolutionary science

Kuhn claimed that for the most part scientists operate within the prevailing paradigm, accepting its assumptions unquestioningly and conducting "normal science." They refine existing theories, apply them to new situations, seek to explain puzzling data and improve experimental techniques.

But over time insoluble problems arise, or experimental data accumulate which can't be reconciled with existing theories. Eventually these difficulties lead to a crisis that prompts a scientific revolution and the adoption of a new paradigm.

The new paradigm is able to explain the data that the old paradigm explained, account for anomalies, and predict and explain new phenomena. It also throws up new questions, opens up new avenues of exploration, and sets new rules for conducting research.

Once the new paradigm has become well-established, normal science resumes.

incommensurability

Controversially, Kuhn claimed that there are no objective means of choosing between competing paradigms. Each paradigm has its own world-view, and its own approved ways of conducting investigations and interpreting data.

This means that paradigms are "incommensurable," meaning there is no common basis or standard by which they can be compared. So we can never be sure that science really is progressing with the adoption of a new paradigm. Things may be lost as well as gained.

Adherents of a new paradigm will feel sure that progress has been made since the new paradigm will appear to address some of the shortcomings of the old one.

choosing between theories

Kuhn identified five characteristics of a good scientific theory:

- accuracy
- consistency
- scope
- simplicity
- fruitfulness

Crucially, he said that conflicts may arise when using these criteria to choose between competing theories. For example, one theory might give very accurate results; another may be less accurate but have a wider scope; another might possess elegant simplicity; and so on.

By this account, choosing between competing theories isn't a straightforward matter of seeing which best fits "the evidence." It is a far more complex and subjective matter.

Furthermore, over time, science will solve more and more problems. So, in that sense, progress will occur. But, Kuhn claimed, there is no independent viewpoint from which to judge whether a new paradigm is objectively better or more "true" than an old one.

science & philosophy

Can scientific method be applied to philosophical problems? According to some contemporary philosophers the answer is yes.

Science is our most reliable source of knowledge about the world. Consequently, it enjoys a special status in our society.

scientism
People are generally disposed to accept as true any claim that science corroborates, and to treat with suspicion any claim that science calls into question or cannot corroborate.

Some philosophers, however, think that this veneration for science is sometimes carried too far, that science enjoys too privileged a status, and that scientific method is often applied to situations where it isn't really applicable. It isn't that these philosophers don't respect science—far

from it. But they criticize what they consider to be a tendency for science to overstep its bounds.

Philosophers who take this view use the term "scientism" to label what they see as a too-reverential, too-partisan attitude toward science and its methods.

In his 1991 book *Scientism: Philosophy and the Infatuation with Science*, the contemporary philosopher Tom Sorell defines scientism as "a matter of putting too high a value on science in comparison with other branches of learning or culture."

In these contexts, scientism is used as a pejorative term to label a view that is judged to place "too high a value" on science.

But scientism needn't be used as a term of abuse. It can also be used in a purely descriptive sense to refer to the view that science is the most authoritative and valuable part of human knowledge.

Scientism comes in two varieties. "Strong scientism" is the view that scientific knowledge is the only genuine kind of knowledge, and that only scientific claims are meaningful. "Weak scientism" is the view that science is by far the best source of knowledge, and that scientific method can and should be applied to other disciplines, including the humanities and social sciences.

philosophical questions
Many of the questions that have traditionally interested philosophers don't appear to lend themselves to scientific investigation. For example, questions about

how we ought to live, the existence of God and the nature of knowledge.

If strong scientism is true then knowledge of such matters would seem to be impossible. If weak scientism is true then any knowledge that can be gained of such matters must be vastly inferior to scientific knowledge.

Unsurprisingly, many philosophers reject scientism. They claim that there are some questions that can't be investigated scientifically, but which are worthy of investigation nonetheless. Such questions can be investigated through the methods of philosophy, and meaningful answers can be found.

naturalism

Some contemporary philosophers, however, take the opposite view. They believe that scientific knowledge *is* the only genuine form of knowledge, and that only scientific claims *are* meaningful.

They adopt an approach to philosophy known as "naturalism," which holds that there is no special method of philosophy distinct from scientific method, and no special philosophical knowledge distinct from scientific knowledge.

Naturalists hold that every being and every event in the universe is part of the natural world, and is, in principle, open to investigation by the natural sciences. This,

self-defeating?

Critics of strong scientism often claim that it's self-defeating. Their argument runs as follows:

According to strong scientism, only scientific claims are meaningful. But this isn't a scientific claim, it's a philosophical one. Therefore, according to strong scientism, strong scientism is itself meaningless.

of course, includes humans and all their thoughts, actions, and concerns. They believe that traditional philosophical problems need to be reformulated so that they can be investigated scientifically. For example, the traditional epistemological quest for an ultimate grounding for knowledge ought be replaced by a psychological investigation into how scientific knowledge is gained and used.

Traditionally, philosophical theories have been regarded as untestable by observation (pages 12–15). But naturalists say otherwise. If they're right (and that's a very big "if") then the future of philosophy is science.

glossary

a posteriori Latin, "from the latter"; a proposition is known *a posteriori* if it is known on the basis of experience.

a priori Latin, "from the earlier"; a proposition is known *a priori* if it is known independently of experience.

ad hominem the fallacy of attacking someone's character or circumstances rather than the soundness of their arguments.

aesthetics the branch of philosophy dealing with art, beauty and taste.

antecedent in logic, the bit following the "if" in an "if … then …" statement.

applied ethics the branch of philosophy that applies ethical theories to specific moral problems. *See also* normative ethics.

argument a statement or set of statements in support of a conclusion. *See also* deductive argument, invalid argument, inductive argument, invalid argument, ontological argument.

assumption in logic, a proposition that is accepted as true as a starting point for reasoning.

behaviorism in philosophy, the view that the mind is nothing above and beyond behavior.

categorical imperative in the ethical system of Immanuel Kant, an absolute moral obligation.

cogito shorthand name used for Descartes' famous dictum, *cogito ergo sum* (see below).

cogito ergo sum dictum coined by René Descartes; Latin for "I think, therefore I exist."

coherentism the theory of truth according to which a belief is true if it coheres with a system of other beliefs.

consequent in logic, the bit following the "then" in an "if … then …" statement.

consequentialism the ethical view that the rightness or wrongness of actions is to be judged by their consequences.

contradiction a logical incompatibility between two or more propositions.

cosmological argument an argument in which the existence of God is inferred from observable facts, or alleged facts, about the universe.

deduction a process of reasoning whereby the conclusion follows necessarily from the premises.

deductive argument an argument that is intended to be deductively valid.

deontology an approach to ethics that focusses on adhering to moral duties.

dialectic a method of discussing and examining different viewpoints to arrive at the truth.

dialogue in philosophy, a conversation in which various viewpoints are argued back and forth in an attempt to advance closer to the truth.

dilemma, constructive the name of a valid rule of inference in propositional logic whereby if P implies Q and R implies S and either P or R is true, then Q or S has to be true.

dilemma, destructive the name of a valid rule of inference in propositional logic whereby if P implies Q and R implies S and either Q is false or S is false, then either P or R must be false.

disjunctive statement a statement of the form "either … or …."

dualism in philosophy of mind, the view that the mind and body are two radically different kinds of thing.

empiricism the epistemological doctrine that all knowledge is derived from sense-experience.

epiphenomenalism the view that mental events are caused by physical events in the brain, but that mental events have no effect on physical events.

epistemology the branch of philosophy concerned with the validity and limits of knowledge.

esse is percipi "to be is to be perceived," the central principle of George Berkeley's idealism.

ethics the branch of philosophy that deals with questions concerning what is good and bad, and what is right and wrong. *See also* metaethics.

eudaimonia the term used by Aristotle to denote a state of happiness and flourishing.

ex falso quodlibet the medieval name for a rule of inference which allows you to deduce anything from contradictory premises, also known as the "principle of explosion."

fallacy an argument based on a false or invalid inference.

falsification in the philosophy of science, the act of showing, or attempting to show, that a theory is wrong.

felicific calculus a method, devised by Jeremy Bentham, for working out the total amount of pleasure resulting from an action.

foundationalism the epistemological doctrine that certain basic beliefs must be known before other truths can be known.

functionalism in the philosophy of mind, the view that mental states are defined by their functional roles, by what they do rather than what they are made from.

golden mean in Aristotle's ethics, the virtuous middle-ground between two non-virtuous extremes.

hedonism the ethical doctrine that pleasure is the only good.

hypothetical syllogism a type of deductive argument that has a conditional statement (an "if … then …" statement) for one or more of its premises.

idealism philosophical viewpoint that reality is ultimately mental rather than physical.

immaterialism a metaphysical doctrine denying the existence of matter.

induction a process of reasoning which moves from a limited number of individual observations to a general conclusion.

inductive argument an argument based upon inductive reasoning.

infallibilism the epistemological view that knowledge is limited to true beliefs that cannot rationally be doubted.

inference a conclusion drawn from evidence and reasoning.

invalid argument an argument in which the truth of the premises does not entail the truth of the conclusion. *See also* valid argument.

logic the branch of philosophy concerned with principles of correct reasoning.

materialism the view that reality consists of material objects.

maxim in the philosophy of Immanuel Kant, the principles or intentions that guide a person's actions.

metaethics the branch of ethics concerned with questions about the nature of ethics itself.

metaphysics branch of philosophy concerned with the ultimate nature of being, or the general nature of reality.

method of doubt the process used by Descartes for rejecting all beliefs for which there is the slightest possibility of error.

modus ponens a valid argument form, also known as affirming the antecedent.

modus tollens a valid argument form, also known as denying the consequent.

monad in Leibniz's metaphysics, a non-material soul-like substance.

moral realism the ethical view that there are objective moral facts.

moral relativism the ethical view that morality is culturally based and that there are no absolute standards of right and wrong.

natural numbers the numbers used for counting 1, 2, 3, 4, … .

natural philosophy natural science, especially physical science.

natural theology religion based on evidence as opposed to faith.

naturalism in ethics, the theory that ethical terms can be derived from non-ethical ones.

naturalistic fallacy the alleged fallacy of treating ethical terms as though they were descriptions of natural properties.

normative ethics the branch of philosophy that attempts to establish the standards of right and wrong. *See also* applied ethics.

occasionalism the metaphysical doctrine that there is no interaction between mind and body, but that God makes mental and physical events correspond to one another.

ontological argument proof for the existence of God based purely upon the definition of God.

ontology the branch of metaphysics that studies the nature of existence, or being.

paraconsistent logic nonclassic systems of logic that attempt to deal with contradictions without lapsing into absurdity.

paradigm in philosophy of science, a philosophical and theoretical framework in which scientific research is conducted.

paradox an argument that appears to generate a contradiction or absurdity.

parallelism the view that mental and physical phenomena occur in parallel but are not causally linked.

physicalism a philosophical viewpoint that everything that exists is ultimately physical.

polymath a person of great learning or expertise in multiple fields of study.

premise a proposition upon which an argument is based or a conclusion is drawn.

problem of consciousness the difficulty that materialism has with accounting for the subjective aspect of mental experience.

relativism *see* moral relativism

representative realism the view that we do not perceive objects directly, but only indirectly through mental images or representations.

scientism the view that only scientific claims are meaningful.

syllogism a kind of argument, in which deductive reasoning is used to reach a conclusion based on two or more propositions that are assumed to be true.

teleological argument argument for the existence of God based on the perceived evidence of design in the physical world.

theism the belief that an all-powerful, all-knowing, supremely good creator.

trademark argument argument for the existence of God, devised by Descartes, based on the fact that we have an idea of God.

tripartite theory of knowledge the view that knowledge is true justified belief.

utilitarianism an ethical doctrine that bases the moral worth of an action on the amount of happiness it produces.

valid argument an argument in which the truth of the premises entails the truth of the conclusion. *See also* invalid argument.

virtue a trait of character which is considered good or excellent.

bibliography

Annas, Julia, *Ancient Philosophy: A Very Short Introduction* (Oxford University Press, 2000)

Anselm, *Proslogion: With the Replies of Gaunilo and Anselm* (Hackett Publishing Co., 2001)

Aquinas, Thomas (translator, Timothy McDermott), *Selected Philosophical Writings* (Oxford University Press, 2008)

Aristotle (translator, Terence H. Irwin), *Nicomachean Ethics* (Hackett Publishing Co, 2nd edition 2000)

Ayer, A. J., *The Problem of Knowledge* (Penguin Books, 1990)

Baggini, Julian, *Atheism: A Very Short Introduction* (Oxford University Press, 2003)

Barnes, Jonathan, *Aristotle: A Very Short Introduction* (Oxford University Press, 2000)

Berkeley, George, *Principles of Human Knowledge and Three Dialogues Between Hylas and Philonous* (Penguin Classics, 1988)

Chalmers, A. F. *What is this Thing Called Science?* (Oxford University Press, third edition 1999)

Descartes, René (translator, Ian Maclean), *A Discourse on the Method* (Oxford University Press, 2008)

Descartes, René (translator, Michael Moriarty), *Meditations on First Philosophy* (Oxford World's Classics, 2008)

Driver, Julia, *Ethics: The Fundamentals* (Wiley-Blackwell, 2006)

Epicurus (translator John K. Strodach) *The Art of Happiness* (Penguin Classics, 2013)

Feser, Edward, *Philosophy of Mind: A Beginner's Guide* (Oneworld Publications, 2006)

Francks, Richard, *Modern Philosophy: The Seventeenth and Eighteenth Centuries* (Routledge, 2003)

Hayden, Gary, *The Bedside Book of Paradoxes* (New Burlington Books, 2014)

Hayden, Gary, *You Kant Make It Up: Strange Ideas from History's Greatest Philosophers* (Oneworld, 2011)

Honderich, Ted (editor), *The Oxford Companion to Philosophy* (Oxford University Press, second edition 2005)

Hume, David, *Dialogues Concerning Natural Religion* (Oxford World's Classics, 2008)

Hume, David, *An Enquiry Concerning Human Understanding* (Oxford University Press, 2008)

Hume, David, *A Treatise on Human Nature: Being an Attempt to Introduce the Experimental Method of Reasoning into Moral Subjects* (Penguin Classics, 1985)

Kenny, Anthony, *A New History of Western Philosophy* (Oxford University Press, 2012)

Kuhn, Thomas, *The Structure of Scientific Revolutions* (University of Chicago Press, new and revised edition 1996)

Ladyman, James, *Understanding the Philosophy of Science* (Routledge, 2001)

Leibniz, G. W., *Discourse on Metaphysics and The Monadology* (Dover Publications, 2005)

Locke, John, *An Essay Concerning Human Understanding* (Penguin Classics, 1997)

Mackie, J. L., *The Miracle of Theism: Arguments For and Against the Existence of God* (Oxford University Press, 1983)

Madsen, Pirai, *How to Win Every Argument: the Use and Abuse of Logic* (Bloomsbury Academic, second edition 2015)

Magee, Bryan, *Confessions of a Philosopher: A Journey through Western Philosophy* (Modern Library, 1999)

Maslin, K. T., *Introduction to the Philosophy of Mind* (Polity, second edition 2007)

Meister, Chad, *Introducing the Philosophy of Religion* (Routledge, 2009)

Mill, John Stuart and Bentham, Jeremy, *Utilitarianism and Other Essays* (Pearson, 2000)

Okasha, Samir, *Philosophy of Science: A Very Short Introduction* (Oxford University Press, 2002)

Paley, William, *Natural Theology* (Oxford University Press, 2008)

Panza, Christopher and Potthast, Adam, *Ethics for Dummies* (John Wiley, 2010)

Plato (editor, David Gallop), *Defence of Socrates, Euthyphro, Crito* (Oxford World's Classics, 2008)

Plato (translators, Harold Tarrant and Hugh Tredennick) *The Last Days of Socrates* (Penguin Classics, 2003)

Plato (translator, Desmond Lee), *Republic* (Penguin Books, 1987)

Plato (translator, Robin Waterfield), *Thaetetus* (Penguin Classics, 1987)

Priest, Graham, *Logic: A Very Short Introduction* (Oxford University Press, 2000)

Pritchard, Duncan, *What is this Thing Called Knowledge?* (Routledge, third edition, 2013)

Russell, Bertrand, *History of Western Philosophy* (Routledge, new edition 2004)

Russell, Bertrand, *The Problems of Philosophy* (Oxford University Press, 2001)

Ryle, Gilbert, *The Concept of Mind* (Penguin Classics, 2000)

Sainsbury, R. M., *Paradoxes* (Cambridge University Press, third edition 2011)

Scruton, Roger, *Kant: A Very Short Introduction* (Oxford University Press, 2001)

Singer, Peter, *Animal Liberation* (Pimlico, 1995)

Sorell, Tom, *Scientism: Philosophy and the Infatuation with Science* (Routledge, new edition 1994)

Spinoza, Benedict (translator, Edwin Curley), *Ethics* (Penguin Classics, 1996)

Velasquez, Manuel, *Philosophy: A Text with Readings* (Wadsworth Publishing Co., 2013)

Warburton, Nigel, *Philosophy: the Basics* (Routledge, fifth edition, 2012)

Warburton, Nigel, *Thinking from A to Z* (Routledge, third edition 2007)

suggested reading

If you're keen to learn more about philosophy, but unsure where to go to next, here are some recommendations.

books

A Little History of Philosophy by Nigel Warburton
(Yale University Press, 2012)
A brief, breezy, but informative romp through the history of Western philosophy.

History of Western Philosophy by Bertrand Russell
(Routledge, new edition 2004)
A beautifully written, intellectually stimulating introduction to history's great philosophers and their ideas. A classic.

The Last Days of Socrates by Plato
(Penguin Classics, 2010)
Contains four of Plato's best dialogues, "Euthyphro," "Apology," "Crito," and "Phaedo." The perfect introduction to the works of history's most celebrated philosopher.

Meditations on First Philosophy by René Descartes
(Oxford World Classics, 2008)
One of the most important philosophical works of all time. Short and compelling. A must-read.

Modern Philosophy: the Seventeenth and Eighteenth Centuries by Richard Francks
(McGill-Queen's University Press, 2003)
A superb introduction to a fascinating period of philosophy. Explains the ideas of Descartes, Spinoza, Leibniz, Locke, Berkeley, and Hume with admirable and easy-going clarity.

Think: A Compelling Introduction to Philosophy by Simon Blackburn
(Oxford Paperbacks, 1999)
A brief introduction to some of philosophy's biggest questions. It's designed to make you think, and therefore quite a challenging read. But worth the effort.

online resources (free)

Stanford Encyclopedia of Philosophy
Plato.stanford.edu
Has a wealth of in-depth and authoritative articles on all aspects of philosophy. Maintained by Stanford University.

History of Philosophy Without Any Gaps
historyofphilosophy.net
Presented by Professor Peter Adamson of King's College, London. Jaw-droppingly good and extensive collection of fun and informative podcasts. An excellent first-stop for gaining an overview of any major philosopher's life and works.

Philosophy Bites
philosophybites.com
Presented by Nigel Warburton and David Edmonds. A podcast series featuring 20-minute interviews with top philosophers, on a variety of topics.

index

acknowledgments

© Alamy | Geoff A Howard 15

© Creative Commons 49

© Getty Images | De Agostini Picture Library 76 | National Galleries of Scotland 83 | Bill Pierce 180

© Shutterstock | Adya 59 | Africa Studio 41 | Alan Poulson Photography 158 | Alliance 99 | anekoho 95 | anigoweb 152 | Anna Omelchenko 130 | Anna Rassadnikova 149 | Antlio 73 | ArtHeart 143 | Asmus Koefoed 97 | Babin 86 | best works 183 | bikeriderlondon 119 | bioraven 33 | Brendan Howard 65 | Cat_arch_angel 34 | Chirtsova Natalia 33 | CLIPAREA l Custom media 147 | cristi180884 141 | Darren Pullman 69 | DCornelius 143 | djgis 105 | Dragon Images 158 | easyshoot 92 | EdgeOfReason 65 | eveleen 103, 157 | Evgeny Dubinchuk 143 | ER_09 106 | Falko Matte 56, 70 | Fedorov Oleksiy 132 | Garsya 156 | Gergely Zsolnai 90 | Gemenacom 150 | Givaga 51 | graphixmania 128 | Hein Nouwens 49, 78, 129 | imagineerinx 137 | Inga Nielsen 123 | Itana 118 | Jan Kaliciak 36 | Jenny Lilly 117| Jiri Hera 31, 41 | Julian Rovagnati 157 | Kjolak 90 | KoQ Creative 86, 105 | LanKS 102 | Lightspring p.151 | Ljupco Smokovski 124 | LuckyImages 95 | lynea 24, 60, 135, 149 | M. Unal Ozmen 103 | MaKars 96 | Marafona 148, 157 | mariait p.60 | mart 60 | MastakA 113 | Marzolino 13, 67 | Matjaz Preseren 27, 34 | Minerva Studio 121 | Modfos 33 | moj0j0 89 | Mopic 144 | Morphart Creation 89, 95, 105, 130 | musicman 90 | Nicku 70 | Nitr 96 | Ociacia 155 | Oleksandr Rybitskiy 101 | Ollyy 62, 147 | Photobank gallery 17 | Photology1971 128 | Pixel Embargo 50 | ppart 135 | Radu Bercan 148 | Rawpixel.com 102 | robert_s 69 | Robert Adrian Hillman 117, 124 | RTimages 10, 17 | seeyou 102 | Sergey Goryachev 34 | Sergey Nivens 88, 153 | soft_light 62 | Sonchai Suphanpipat 68 | song_mi 101 | Stankevich 63 | studioVin 151 | TANANKA ALENA 150 | ThavornC 150 | theromb 158 | Thomas Pajot 157 | Thumbelina 111 | Tim UR 159 | Titima Ongkantong 86 | Triff 13 | valzan 84 | Vasilius 28 | Viacheslav Lopatin 93 | Voropaev Vasiliy 135 | wavebreakmedia 62 | yoeml 108 | Zlatko Guzmic 142 | Zora Rossi 49

All other images are in the public domain.

Every effort has been made to credit the copyright holders of the images used in this book. We apologize for any unintentional omissions or errors and will insert the appropriate acknowledgment to any companies or individuals in subsequent editions of the work.